START A
REVOLUTION

START
A REVO
LUTION
STOP ACTING LIKE A LIBRARY

BEN BIZZLE
with Maria Flora

ala
editions

AN IMPRINT OF THE AMERICAN LIBRARY ASSOCIATION
CHICAGO I 2015

ISBNs
978-0-8389-1267-6 (paper)
978-0-8389-1282-9 (PDF)
978-0-8389-1283-6 (ePub)
978-0-8389-1284-3 (Kindle)

Library of Congress Cataloging-in-Publication Data
Bizzle, Ben.
  Start a revolution : stop acting like a library / Ben Bizzle with Maria Flora.
    pages   cm
  Includes bibliographical references and index.
  ISBN 978-0-8389-1267-6 (paperback)
  1. Libraries—United States—Marketing—Case studies. 2. Libraries—Public relations—United States—Case studies. 3. Public libraries—Information technology—United States—Case studies. 4. Libraries and community—United States—Case studies. 5. Craighead County and Jonesboro Public Library (Ark.) 6. Public libraries—Arkansas. I. Flora, Maria. II. Title.
  Z716.3.B57 2015
  021.70973—dc23   2014028826

Cover design by Ben Bizzle. Text design and composition by Pauline Neuwirth in the Minion Pro and Trade Gothic Lt Std typefaces.

♾ This paper meets the requirements of ANSI/NISO Z39.48–1992 (Permanence of Paper).

Printed in the United States of America

19 18 17 16 15   5 4 3 2 1

*Dedicated to Phyllis Burkett
without whom none of this would ever have happened*

CONTENTS

FOREWORD

It's been said that when Walt Disney was casting for the first *Mickey Mouse Club* TV show he didn't want professionals. He advised the staff not to go to talent agents to find Mouseketeers, "Go to a school and watch what happens to you. You'll notice that you're watching one kid. Not any of the other kids, but sooner or later your gaze will always go back to this one kid. That kid has star quality."

Ben Bizzle is that kid.

I met Ben in 2012 when my dear friend and librarian extraordinaire, Janie Hermann of Princeton Public Library, and I were moderating a marketing track at the "Computers in Libraries" conference. After one of the sessions he showed us the billboards his library had created and we immediately wanted him to present for our track. Now mind you, it took us months to come up with that program. We were certain we had lined up the best marketing ideas and speakers in the library field and yet it took us all of five minutes listening to Ben to add him to the venue.

That's the impact Ben has on people.

He's smart, insightful, and funny. The excitement and energy he puts into his projects are contagious. Like me, he came to the library field as an outsider with neither library experience nor an MLS, and fell in love with the people, purpose, and possibilities that libraries can offer their communities. He is a brazen storyteller who will make you laugh, cry, and cringe. He sees problems as puzzles that need to be solved and is always generous whether he is sharing the credit or figuring out a way to share his ideas with others.

That's Ben.

This is an important book, not just for marketers, but for anyone who wonders how successful libraries do it. This is the real story—not the one we write up for awards or tell once everything is said and done. No, this tells it like it is, with all the bumps and bruises that successful libraries encounter on their path of progress. It tells the story of how courage and collaboration contribute to success; the importance of leaders who let others lead; and what happens when libraries listen to their communities. He'll tell you how to do everything his library did, but you'll have to pay attention to the bigger story if you really want to find success.

Ben likes to say he's just a tech guy who knows a little about people. I say he's the guy who wrote the book that just might start a revolution.

NANCY DOWD
Coauthor of *Bite-Sized Marketing:*
Realistic Solutions for Overworked Librarians
The 'M' Word Blog

ACKNOWLEDGMENTS

True friends stab you in the front.
—OSCAR WILDE

THESE ARE THE people who inspire me, motivate me, challenge me, and keep me honest. I'm not always an easy person to deal with, and these people love me anyway.

I need to begin by thanking Maria Flora for helping me organize all the jumbled thoughts in my head and teaching me how to "write my voice." I could have never written this book without you. While there, I want to thank John Flora for loaning me his wife to work on this project. Also, thank you to Carson Block, Ned Potter, and Josh Tate for your contributions to this work. And thank you to Nancy Dowd for writing a foreword that makes me sound better than I could ever hope to be.

Thank you to Morgan Sallee for supporting and tolerating me during this process. You are a beautiful soul and I'll always love you. Thanks to my mom, Kathy Ray, for letting me vent my frustrations to her, and then offering her compassionate words of wisdom, "Ben, quit whining and just finish the damn book." I finally finished it, mom. And a very special thank you to Joe Box, my best friend and partner in crime throughout this journey. You give me the courage to do things I probably shouldn't do.

Thank you to Brandi Hodges, Valerie Carroll, Melloney Dunlap, Micah Brightwell, Nina Darley, Wade Brightwell, and Sarah Stuart. You folks are the creative team. I'm just the guy with the big mouth. Thank you to all of my coworkers at Craighead County Jonesboro Public Library. You are a family to me in a way you will never know. And you remind me that I'm still just the guy who hasn't fixed your printer yet. I wrote this book, but you did this work. This is your book, not mine.

Thank you to all the people in the library industry who have been friends and inspirations to me: Carolyn Ashcraft, David Lee King, Sarah Houghton, Emily Clasper, Patrick Sweeney, J. P. Porcaro, John Chrastka, Kathy Dempsey, Janie Hermann, Rebekkah Smith Aldrich, Sue Considine, Stacie Ledden, Stephen Abram, Jane Dysart, Kevin Smith, Jenny Levine, Nicolette

Sosulski, Nina McHale, and so many others I know I'm leaving off. I'd like to particularly thank Jeannie Allen for coming up with the idea of the "Library Dropbox." Thank you to the members of ALA Think Tank. I admire the passion, brilliance, and commitment you show every day, as you share ideas and give of yourselves to make our industry better.

Finally, I want to thank David Eckert for fostering an environment of creativity and providing us with the security to fail with confidence. You are a true leader.

THE JONESBORO STORY

WRITE A BOOK?

It was about 11:15 on the morning of Wednesday, October 24, 2012. Melloney Dunlap, our graphic designer at Craighead County Jonesboro Public Library, and I had just finished our first national presentation at the Internet Librarian conference in Monterey, California. Our presentation, "Marketing on the Edge," was about the technology and marketing strategies we had implemented at our library. We'd gotten quite a bit of attention over the previous few months for our "Meme Your Library" ad campaign, a series of humorous posters, postcards, and billboards we created using the popular Internet eCard meme as a template. But we'll get to all of that later. Suffice it to say, the presentation went well. People really seemed to embrace the idea of using humor as an effective way for a library to engage the community.

As we were gathering our things, a few people came up to the stage to ask questions or comment on the presentation. Once everyone else had left to go to their next sessions, a woman approached and handed me her card, introducing herself as a representative for a publishing company. She asked if I'd ever considered writing a book about the things we'd just presented. Initially, I thought she was joking. I'd been a wreck two hours earlier, letting my nerves get the better of me at the prospect of presenting in front of a few hundred people. I knew the presentation had gone pretty well, but the idea that anyone would actually want to read a book about our library just seemed ridiculous. So, naturally, I told her I'd think about it.

IN THE BEGINNING

Let's back up a bit. In March 2008, I saw an ad in a newspaper that the Craighead County Jonesboro Public Library was looking for a technology director. After seven years of managing technology in a hospital, where emergencies were literally life and death, working in a library sounded pretty refreshing. I submitted my resume and was called in for an interview.

I was met by David Eckert and Phyllis Burkett. David was the assistant library director and had just started in December 2007. He was an enthusiastic guy who laughed kind of loud and talked a lot. Phyllis had been the director of the library for twenty-eight years. She epitomized every stereo-type I ever had about what a librarian looked like. Both were very person-able, and our interview lasted for more than three hours. It had been more of a relaxed conversation than an actual interview, until, near the end, when Phyllis looked at me very seriously and asked, "Do you have what it takes to take this library to the next level?"

I didn't have any idea what she was talking about. When I walked into that interview I didn't even have a library card. I didn't know what level the library was on or what the next level looked like. But I did know the answer to that interview question. I confidently assured her that I abso-lutely had what it took to take this library to the next level.

In May 2008 I became the director of technology at the Craighead County Jonesboro Public Library (CCJPL) in Arkansas. On my first day of work, I met Joe Box, the systems administrator who had just started in January. Upon our initial introduction, I felt like David and Phyllis had intentionally kept us from meeting before I accepted the position.

Joe was wearing a black T-shirt, baggy jeans, and combat boots. I was wearing a green and pink-striped Polo, khaki pants, and dress shoes. He had a full beard, a receding hairline with a long ponytail running down his back, big steel rings in his ears, and a pierced eyebrow. I was standing there, clean-shaven, multiple hair care products in my hair, and my sun-glasses perched on top of my head. Joe was in his mid-twenties and looked like someone you'd warn your daughter about. I was in my mid-thirties and looked like someone's middle-aged dad.

As I reached to shake his hand, all I could think was, "Oh God. He's one of *those* guys."

And as he stood and shook my hand, all he could think was, "Oh God. He's one of *those guys*."

Thus began a wonderful friendship. We came to appreciate each other's intellect, technical savvy, and brutal sense of humor. It's hard to call it work when you geek out on computers and crack jokes with your best friend every day. But they keep paying us for it, so we keep showing up.

IF YOU BUILD IT, THEY WILL COME

Our predecessors in the Information Technology (IT) Department had built the library's technology infrastructure using a lot of open source software. Things like e-mail, content filtering, user management, and connectivity required constant maintenance. Our first year at the library was spent rebuilding the infrastructure at all our branch libraries, installing a new mail server, and putting security measures in place to resolve issues with spam, viruses, and Internet content filtering.

In March 2009 David Eckert, our assistant director, and I went to the "Computers in Libraries" conference in Washington, DC. Until then, Joe and I had been working on technology upgrades that weren't necessarily library-related. With neither of us having any background in libraries, we were still learning about the technologies specific to the industry. But "Computers in Libraries" would change all that. It was my first opportunity to hear how other professionals were integrating technologies into the library environment.

I specifically remember David Lee King's session about website design. He was talking about the user experience and how important it was that we not only provide access to library resources, but also create a digital environment that is easy to navigate and aesthetically appealing. He definitely wasn't talking about our website at CCJPL. It was neither easy to navigate, nor aesthetically appealing.

By 2009, our library's website was already several years old. It consisted of page after page of links, text, and clip art, without much structure to any of it. Some of the links worked and most of the words were spelled correctly. As is the case in many libraries, our website was a little-used afterthought. It provided basic information about the library branches, had a calendar of events, and linked to several research databases. There was no other digital content and the only interactivity available was an e-mail address where patrons could e-mail the library.

After getting approval from the board, Joe and I formed a staff committee from the various departments in the library and began working with a local web development company on a new website. We decided we wanted to design the sight similar to the websites of online news outlets. The news media and libraries share the common challenge of providing significant amounts of information and making that information quickly and easily accessible to the general public.

Utilizing images and graphics to catch users' attention, a menu structure that made accessing information throughout the site fast and intuitive, and a new content management system that made updating the site easy for staff, our focus was on simplicity of access. (See figure P.1.)

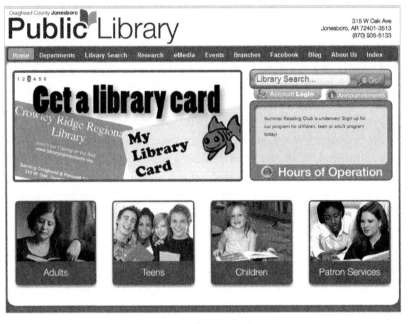

FIGURE P.1
CCJPL 2009 website redesign

We launched our new website on December 1, 2009. Shortly after launching the website, we signed a contract with OverDrive to provide e-books and audiobooks to our patrons. With the availability of e-books and audiobooks as its centerpiece, the new website was our first step in tearing down the walls of the library. We were breaking away from the perception of the library as just a building full of books. We were becoming a provider of digital information and entertainment and reaching into the homes of our patrons.

In 2010 we turned our attention to the mobile environment and began development of a mobile website for the library. We'd witnessed the explosion of smartphones and knew our next step in expanding the library's reach was to develop a mobile presence. Our process for creating the mobile site was very similar to the approach we used to develop our main website. We again formed a committee and started discussing what services we could provide in the mobile environment. Our focus was now on extending our digital reach beyond our patrons' homes and into their hands, wherever they might be.

OverDrive already had a mobile website and app available, so it was a natural choice for the platform. We also purchased Airpac, the mobile catalog available through our ILS vendor, Innovative Interfaces. We worked to integrate as much device functionality as possible into the site, as well. The e-mail addresses, phone numbers, and addresses of our branches were all linked, so that with a single tap, patrons could e-mail, call, text, or get directions to our locations. We went with a simple layout, again attempting to create a clean and unintimidating user experience for our patrons. Our mobile site launched on August 11, 2010.

A couple of months later we looked into a service called Freegal Music, which provided downloadable MP3s that patrons could keep forever. While they didn't provide a mobile app for the service until 2012, we were still able to integrate a link to the Freegal site onto our mobile website, adding music to the collection of digital services we were providing on multiple platforms.

By the end of 2010, we had created a robust digital environment for our patrons. In just over a year, we'd gone from no significant digital presence at all to offering a wide range of library services on multiple platforms. In 2009 virtually no one was visiting the library's old website. Since launching the new site in December of that year, we've had over 1,100,000 visits to our website. Our mobile site has received over 125,000 visits.

The impact, however, wasn't immediate. It took time to make the public aware of our web presence and digital services. During its first year, our mobile website averaged 20 visits per day. Today, it averages 138. Mobile traffic now makes up over 30 percent of our website traffic. The growth patterns in usage of our e-books, audiobooks, and music have been similar. We delivered 4,618 e-books and audiobooks to patrons during our first contract year with OverDrive. In 2013, 41,834 titles were downloaded. Likewise, in our first year of offering music through Freegal, patrons downloaded 10,836 songs, compared to 38,052 in 2013.

I'd like to be able to say we foresaw all of this, that it was part of some long-term technology strategy, but that simply wasn't the case. In 2009 we had a bad website and wanted to create a better one, believing it would help us better serve our community. The growth rate of our digital library has exceeded even our loftiest expectations. In the process, it has become as integral to our success as any of our physical offerings. It is simultaneously an entity unto itself and a digital representation of who we are as an organization.

ADVERTISING WHEN ADVERTISING WASN'T COOL

The successes above aren't exclusively a result of the work we were doing technologically. During this process, we were also developing new and creative ways to increase public awareness of the changes taking place at the library.

Prior to 2009, the library had a very traditional approach to community awareness. Without any form of digital outreach, we relied on the promotional approaches still dominant in many libraries today. There was a long-standing relationship with the local newspaper, so stories were written about events at the library or new services we were providing. We also had a constant stack of fliers at the checkout desks, as well as bookmarks, lots of bookmarks. Our "giveaways" were the expected: bags, notepads, and magnets. The problem with these approaches isn't that they're not good. It's that, by and large, they're reaching an audience that already uses the library.

That being said, Library Director Phyllis Burkett, who was responsible for all marketing decisions, had begun to see the value of promoting the library in new ways during the economic recession. Taking advantage of a weak advertising market and understanding the role the library could play in helping our community recover, she hired public relations and graphic design interns from the local college to create "Save Money @ Your Library" promotional materials, including four billboards. This campaign, coupled with an increase in services related to job searching, computer training, and resume review, gave the library the opportunity to assist thousands of patrons during this challenging time. She also saw an opportunity to begin promoting the library at the local movie theater, signing an annual contract for a thirty-second ad that would run on all fifteen screens before every movie, a promotional approach still unheard of in libraries.

Despite the success of these initiatives, there were several limitations with our approach: hiring student interns for public relations and graphic design made it difficult to establish a consistency of voice and public image. Additionally, while Phyllis knew everything about the library and its value to the community, her many other responsibilities limited the time she could devote to working on marketing.

A ROSE BY ANY OTHER NAME

Having built a robust digital library for our patrons, I began encouraging Phyllis to make the public relations (PR) and graphic design positions permanent and full-time, convinced that if we were to continue to grow as an organization, consistency of promotion was going to be integral to our success.

In January 2010 Phyllis went to the library board, proposing the creation of a full-time position for a virtual librarian, a PR role also responsible for maintaining content on the library's website and fledgling Facebook page.

Sometimes, it's the smallest thing than can shape your future. To this day, I believe the job title was the reason the board approved the position. Phyllis was savvy. She realized they weren't likely to approve a full-time public relations position. However, she did believe, correctly, they would support the creation of a librarian-type position to manage our new virtual services, as well as take care of some PR responsibilities.

TIME TO GET CREATIVE

Alissa Reynolds was hired for the position. She was outgoing and creative with a history in sales and management. As the first full-time person responsible for promoting the library, she immediately went to work building community relationships. Early on, she began working with local media, providing opportunities for us to reach out to the community through radio and television, as well as local and state newspapers. We developed new relationships within the business community, thereby increasing sponsorship for library programs and events. This was also the time we began experimenting with social media, started learning how to use Facebook as a marketing tool, and created our own YouTube video series. Having a dedicated, full-time person managing our marketing strategy allowed us to develop consistent marketing campaigns across multiple platforms.

Since the title of the new position was Virtual Librarian and the responsibilities included managing the website content and Facebook page, a close relationship was formed between PR and IT. Considering that we were reaching out in several different mediums, both traditional and digital, we had, by necessity, formed our first, unofficial creative team. We began exploring ways to produce content for the different platforms, which naturally led to discussions, and then brainstorming sessions, about the content itself. We felt that conventional approaches to marketing libraries hadn't made much progress in breaking down the stereotype of libraries as dated institutions. We started exploring different approaches we could use to increase public awareness of all the new services the library had to offer.

BUMPS IN THE ROAD

Unfortunately, in April 2011, Alissa left the library to pursue a different career path. We'd worked hard to convince the board we needed a full-time employee for public relations and were convinced we'd hired the right one. And now she was gone.

It might not have seemed so bad, had we not just lost out graphic design intern a couple of months earlier. We'd been fortunate enough to keep the same graphic design intern for more than just a semester or two. Melloney Dunlap joined the library in December 2008, during her sophomore year of college, doing her college internship as well as working part-time. Having been with the library for over a year, she had begun to establish a consistency in the marketing materials we were producing.

In January 2011, as things were just starting to fall into place, Melloney had to leave her position at the library, as she was finishing her senior year of college and had to focus on school.

Having just launched our mobile site, we were looking forward to promoting all of our new digital services. Our new billboard design was to consist of an image of a smartphone, our web address, and the slogan, "Your library, everywhere you are!" It was a direct message, letting people know that the library was available to them anytime, anywhere.

With Melloney's hiatus, we were forced to bring in a new graphic design intern. Unfortunately, our new intern's style was considerably different than Melloney's and didn't translate well with the material we wanted to produce. The design and approval process were rushed and the billboard did not look good. It was very busy, with too many colors and a bubble font that made the message almost illegible. (See figure P.2.) It was the complete opposite of the simple, clean designs Melloney had been creating. Just as we were beginning to build momentum in promoting all the library's new digital offerings, it seemed as though the wheels were falling off.

While frustrating at the time, the intern situation ultimately worked to our benefit. Initially the board had been resistant to creating a full-time graphic design position. That is, until they saw the contrast in styles between Melloney and the intern we'd been using during her absence. It was

FIGURE P.2
Poorly designed 2011 billboard

clear to them that it was important to have a designer who understood our goals and whose style complemented the library.

In May 2011 the board approved the addition of a full-time graphic designer position, which was immediately offered to Melloney, allowing her to start her professional design career at the library.

LET'S GET THIS PARTY STARTED, FOR REAL THIS TIME

In August 2011 we interviewed and hired Brandi Hodges as the new Virtual Librarian. She fit perfectly with our vision for the role. She was vibrant and articulate, engaging with the public, and already popular in the community. Prior to coming to work for the library, Brandi had spent eight years as a reporter and anchor for KAIT8, our local ABC affiliate. She was also a longtime patron and advocate of the library, having personally experienced the value in the services we offer. Brandi has the type of personality that when she puts a brochure in someone's hand, she does so in a way that makes them want to read it. It had taken almost eight months, but we were finally in a position to start promoting the library the way we had envisioned.

Adding to the strength of our team, Valerie Carroll was hired on at the library in late 2011 in our Information Services Department. She's an exceptional writer and was my original coauthor for this book until she found out she was an expectant mother and had to focus on her new role. Beyond her writing talents, Valerie is passionate about the role the library plays in helping the less fortunate of our community. She's the person who makes sure we never lose sight of the people who need the library the most.

WE'LL CALL IT A CREATIVE TEAM

In January 2012 Melloney told me the billboard company had called and it was time to renew our contract. She wanted to know if I had any ideas for designs. Eager to get rid of the billboards that had been up for the past year, we scheduled a meeting for the following Tuesday at 10:00 a.m. The team that met that morning consisted of Brandi Hodges, Joe Box, Melloney Dunlap, Valerie Carroll, and me. We had all gotten to know each other at the library as well as becoming friends outside of work.

It wasn't by design, but none of us were librarians. In some respects, I think that's turned out to be a benefit. While we worked in a library, we still viewed it largely from the patrons' perspective. We focused more on what the general public might think is cool about the library, and less on what the library might think is cool about itself. We thought about promotion in terms of pulling people in, rather than pushing the library out.

And that's how our creative team was formed. We didn't call ourselves that. We didn't even see ourselves as a team. For our first meeting, which we thought would be our only meeting, we were specifically focused on coming up with billboard ideas. We didn't know we were about to completely change the way we promoted the library. We just wanted to get that ugly billboard down and put something cool in its place.

We tossed around a few ideas and finally decided to use the popular Internet eCard meme as the basis for our billboards. We also decided that instead of having one design that went up on four billboards, we'd come up with four different eCards and have a different design on each board. Since we were going to have to come up with four unique ideas, we decided we would meet again the following week. Each of us would bring five ideas and we'd pick the best ones.

THERE IS NO I IN LIBRARY (WORK WITH ME HERE)

The following week, we got our first taste of just how hard the creative process can be. Not only were a lot of the ideas really bad, but people were getting their feelings hurt when their ideas got shot down. At one point, we stopped talking about billboards and started talking about how we were going to work as a team. It was an important conversation, because we had to decide whether we were going to fight for the best ideas or we were going to fight for our own egos. We collectively agreed to set our emotions aside and be honest with each other. It's natural for us now, but we still had our share of battles early on. We often joke that the most common phrase in our creative team meetings is, "No, that sucks." Most of the ideas we brought to that meeting sucked.

FRUITS OF OUR LABOR

We decided to keep brainstorming and meet again the following week. This time, each of us would bring in ten new ideas. After several hours, we narrowed down over fifty ideas and settled on four. (See figure P.3.)

FIGURE P.3

2012 eCard billboard designs

We met with Phyllis and showed her what we'd come up with. She wasn't familiar with eCards, but she thought the ideas were hilarious. She was always pretty adventurous. She had, after all, been starring in the comedy YouTube videos we'd been making. Once we got her approval on the billboards, we told her that we wanted to extend the eCard theme to include all of the marketing material we created for the year, including posters, bookmarks, and fliers. She agreed to let us meet once a week to work on marketing projects as long as she got to approve anything we came up with. We weren't terribly concerned about gaining her approval. She'd been the one to suggest one of the billboards be, "Book lovers never go to bed alone."

WE MIGHT BE ON TO SOMETHING HERE

Melloney finished the deigns just before Joe and I headed to the 2012 "Computers in Libraries" conference in March and she e-mailed me an image of the four designs she'd sent to the billboard company. It was going to take about three weeks to get them printed and put up.

While we were at the conference in Washington, DC, Joe and I saw that there was an entire track on marketing. We attended one of the morning sessions, a panel discussion led by Janie Hermann, of Princeton Public Library, and Nancy Dowd, product lead for LibraryAware at Novelist. After the session, I went up to the panelists' table and showed them a picture of the billboards we'd created. They loved the designs, showed them to the other panelists, and asked if I'd be willing to spend the last ten minutes of the next session talking about our eCard project. I agreed to do so and sent them a link to the image so they could pull it up on the screen. After Nancy gave me an overly gracious introduction, I talked a bit about our library and creative team. Then I showed the billboards to the people in the audience. People started laughing, taking pictures, and sharing the billboards on Facebook and Twitter. Joe and I suddenly became aware of just how close-knit the library community is. Almost instantly, we became "that library with the billboards." Jennifer Koerber, of Boston Public Library, asked if she could use our billboards the next day in her presentation about humor in libraries. After the session, Nancy and I talked for a few minutes and she told me to let her know if I ever wanted to present about our library's technology and marketing strategies.

FIGURE P.4
Dumbledore billboard

FAME, OR INFAMY?

A couple of weeks later, we got a call from the billboard company that our first billboard was up. It was the Dumbledore "Spoiler Alert" design and was located on the highway coming into town. We all jumped in Melloney's vehicle and headed out to see it. (See figure P.4.)

For the first time, we fully appreciated the remarkable difference between sitting in the office, looking at an image on a computer screen, and standing on the side of the road, looking at a 40-foot billboard. For a brief moment, we all wondered whether this was such a good idea. All of us except Joe, that is. He was too busy laughing hysterically to care that thousands of people were going to see these billboards every day, and that we weren't altogether certain of how they were going to react.

As the summer went on, we continued working on our eCard campaign, creating promotional material for our summer concert series, movie nights, Genealogy Night, and other events. Meanwhile, someone had taken a picture of our Dumbledore billboard and posted it on the social news website, Reddit. To our amazement, it wound up going viral and making the front pages of sites like Reddit and Imgur.

Just after the billboard went viral, we released our "Book Club" YouTube video, which Chuck Palahniuk, author of *Fight Club*, shared through social media. (More on that in the Interlude.)

Then I got a package in the mail from a British friend of mine, Dylan Reece, an amazing chef who works on a luxury yacht in the Mediterranean. Samuel L. Jackson and Magic Johnson had leased the yacht, so he was their chef for a couple of weeks. Dylan showed Samuel L. Jackson a parody Facebook cover I'd created for the library. It was a scene from the movie *Pulp Fiction*. He had Dylan print a copy of it and signed it as only Samuel L. Jackson can. (See figure P.5.)

FIGURE P.5

Samuel L. Jackson called me a bitch, and I'm ok with that

IT'S A NUMBERS GAME

Back in Jonesboro, we couldn't help but laugh at how ridiculous it had all gotten. While Internet virality and acknowledgment from famous people was definitely flattering, it wasn't our objective. Our goal from the beginning was to create promotional material that would get the attention of the people of Jonesboro, Arkansas, and their response had been tremendous. Countless times, people would come into the library or see staff out in the community and comment on one of the posters or billboards they'd seen.

Our utilization and attendance numbers reflected their enthusiasm as well. We host a series of four concerts every summer. It's a Tuesday night event and our average attendance in 2011 was about 100 people at each concert. In 2012, we promoted the series heavily on Facebook and made a different eCard poster for each concert. We hung these posters around town, in bars, restaurants, convenience stores, and anywhere else where we could get permission to hang a poster in a window or on a wall. We averaged over 300 people in attendance at each concert that year. (See figure P.6.)

Our summer movie series had similar success. Publicizing in a similar fashion as we did with our concerts, we saw our attendance increase from 20 people per show to a full capacity crowd of over 60. We went from worrying about whether anyone was going to show up for our programming to having to require registration for some events, just to make sure we could accommodate the numbers in attendance.

We were also seeing exponential increases in utilization of popular services like e-book downloads and free music. Our e-book circulation increased

FIGURE P.6
2012 Summer Concert Series poster

from 8,747 in 2011 to 24,875 in 2012. Similarly, our Freegal music downloads increased from 11,135 in 2011 to 22,705 in 2012. Our circulation of physical materials, new sign-ups for library cards, and daily door traffic were also at record numbers. In three years, from 2009 to 2012, we saw an increase in visitors to the library of over 90 percent, from just over 1,000 patrons a day to over 1,900. Our strategy was working. We were providing better products on more platforms and our aggressive promotional efforts were enticing the community to check out their "new" library.

During this entire time, we'd been steadily increasing our Facebook presence. We had managed to garner just over 4,000 fans by the middle of 2012. We had also been working on our Facebook posting strategies, learning from our experience with our eCard campaign and YouTube videos, and posting a lot of humorous images to our time line. The majority of the growth in our Facebook following was a result of a Facebook ad I had been running for just over a year.

In June 2012 I began working on a new approach to running the library's ad on Facebook. Within a month, we had gained over 800 new fans. Given the success of the test, I wanted to see if the results were universal. Having met some really talented people in the library community, I reached out to a number of libraries and asked if they'd be interested in participating in a case study on Facebook advertising. Seven libraries agreed to participate. I managed a Facebook ad for each library for twenty-eight days, with a spending budget of $10 a day. At the end of twenty-eight days, we'd gained a total of 8,413 fans, an average of 1,201 new fans per library.

SUCCESS WORTH SHARING

Considering the success we were having with our eCard campaign and the results of the Facebook ads trial, I felt we were building promotional strategies that could benefit other libraries as well. I had met Kathy Dempsey, marketing consultant at Libraries Are Essential and author of *The Accidental Library Marketer*, at the ALA Annual Conference in New Orleans in 2011. As it turned out, she and Nancy Dowd were close friends and collaborators on a number of projects. Nancy had mentioned our meeting at "Computers in Libraries," and Kathy contacted me about writing an article for Information Today's *Marketing Library Services* newsletter, for which she was an editor. I agreed to do so and the article was published in the September/October 2012 issue.[1]

I also contacted Nancy and told her I'd be interested in putting together a presentation about our library's marketing strategies. She encouraged me to submit a proposal for the upcoming "Internet Librarian" conference, which is held annually in October in Monterey, California. I submitted a proposal and a few weeks later received an e-mail informing me that it had been accepted. Melloney Dunlap and I were scheduled to present "Marketing on the Edge" on October 24, 2012.

NOW WHERE WAS I?

I apologize. I do tend to get a bit long-winded. I believe I started off talking about a woman approaching me about writing a book. As it turned out, there were three publishers interested in our work. Ultimately, ALA Editions seemed to be the right fit, and here we are today.

Since our first presentation at "Internet Librarian," I've continued to have the privilege of speaking at numerous state and national conferences. And Craighead County Jonesboro Public Library has been honored with a number of awards for our advertising and marketing efforts. Locally, we won two ADDY awards for our eCard campaign. Personally, I was fortunate enough to be awarded the *Library Journal* 2013 "Movers and Shakers" award for marketing, an honor I share with the creative team members, who truly deserve it.

Probably the proudest moment of my library career thus far came when our library received the 2013 John Cotton Dana Library Public Relations Award. The award ceremony was held at the ALA Annual Conference in Chicago on June 30, 2013. That date was also Phyllis's last day as director of our library. After over thirty years of library service, she was retiring. We were fortunate enough to have our entire creative team, as well as Phyllis and Assistant Director David Eckert, on hand for the award ceremony.

When our name was called and we approached the stage to receive our award, I couldn't help but think of our interview five years earlier, when Phyllis gave me that stern look and asked me if I had what it took to take our library to the next level. Our accomplishments weren't anything I could take credit for personally. But together, we really had revolutionized our library. In accepting the award, instead of talking about our marketing campaign, I took the opportunity to talk about Phyllis and her lifelong dedication to libraries. Some things are just more important.

WE'VE ONLY JUST BEGUN . . .

Back at the library, we've continued to build on our successes. The creative team has grown and changed over time. With Nina Darley, youth services coordinator, Wade Brightwell, circulation supervisor, and Sara Stuart of information services joining the team, replacing Joe and Valerie, we've tried to balance the team and ensure representation of all library departments. By the end of 2013, Melloney had accepted a position with a marketing firm and we hired an exceptional young talent in Micah Brightwell to assume the library's graphic design responsibilities.

For our 2013 annual theme, we chose art typography. Having used humor extensively in 2012, we wanted to take a more artistic approach for the following year. While it didn't receive any of the celebrity or Internet attention of the previous year's campaign, it was still effective in spreading our message within our community.

In 2014, unable to resist the urge to again use humor as the primary vehicle for our promotional efforts, our annual campaign theme was Infomercial parody, an idea David had been telling me we should use for almost a year. Given that it was his idea, we even got David to play a leading role in the campaign, as "Library Dave," a Billy Mays impersonation.

The success of our marketing efforts continues to be reflected in our statistics. Our 2013 summer concert series, one of our biggest annual events, saw an increase in attendance of 66 percent over 2012, with an average of over 500 people at each concert. Our e-book circulation increased to over 32,000 downloads, and our music downloads were up 63 percent, with over 37,000 songs downloaded.

Technologically, we contracted with a local web development firm to redesign our website. New technologies would allow us to integrate our mobile and desktop websites into a single, "responsive" site, which would format itself automatically to any screen size. Our new website was launched on June 1, 2013. With it, we've been able to further enhance the delivery of our digital offerings as our patrons continue to move toward mobile platforms. Of the approximately 200,000 annual visits to our website, 30 percent of those visits are now via mobile devices, an increase of 155 percent since 2012.

Our Facebook fan base has grown to over 13,000 and continues to grow at a steady rate. Facebook has proven to be such a successful part of our public awareness efforts that we've expanded our Facebook presence to include pages for our Teen and Children's departments, each of which has over 1,000 fans of its own. Our Facebook posts are seen by over 4,000 people every day, giving us an opportunity to inform our community about the library at a rate never before possible.

We aren't just improving technologically or in our marketing strategies. We continue to look for ways to grow in all areas of our organization. With Phyllis's retirement, David was named as the new library director in a seamless transition of leadership. Rather than hiring an assistant director to fill his now vacant position, he decided to absorb those management responsibilities and created an outreach coordinator position instead. Valerie Carroll was promoted to the position and immediately began working on a comprehensive outreach strategy for the library.

In December 2013 David chose fifteen staff members to participate in a SWOT analysis of our library. SWOT stands for strengths, weaknesses, opportunities, and threats. Over the course of an afternoon, we were able to identify where we saw ourselves strongest and weakest, what our greatest opportunities were to advance as an organization, and what we perceived as the greatest threats to that growth. From customer service and programming to technology and outreach, we are constantly looking for ways to improve the library experience for our community.

WHAT WAS ALL THAT ABOUT?

That's been our story so far at Craighead County Jonesboro Public Library. There hasn't been any one thing that's made the difference in our organization, but a number of interrelated projects that have created a robust library environment for our patrons.

This chapter is meant to provide real-world context for the instructional chapters to follow. It also serves as a case study to use when looking for approval for some of these initiatives within your own library.

The following chapters detail how we re-created our web presence, became an active social media participant within our community, and developed a marketing strategy to increase the public's awareness of the library. The chapters are each meant to serve as individual training guides for implementing these strategies at your library. The bullets at the end of each chapter should be used as talking points when working with decision makers, and implementation checklists once you get their approval.

NOTE

1. Ben Bizzle, "HOW-TO: A Philosophy of Bold Promotion in Arkansas," Information Today, *Marketing Library Services*, September-October 2012, www.infotoday.com/mls/sep12/Bizzle--How-To--A-Philosophy-of-Bold-Promotion-in-Arkansas.shtml.

1

THE DIGITAL LIBRARY

OLD WEBSITE

As I mentioned in the prelude, when I came to work at the library in 2008, the library had no significant online presence. Our website had been designed by a reference librarian several years earlier using a program called Dreamweaver. The site looked very dated. It was uninviting, with clip art for graphics and no real structure. The site was not an accurate representation of who we wanted to be as an organization. It actually had twirling stars on the home page. (See figure 1.1.) We knew redesigning our website had to be one of our first initiatives.

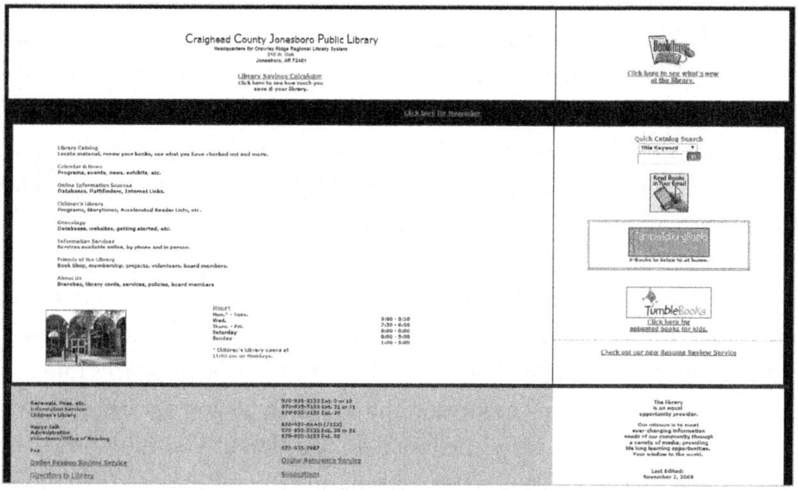

FIGURE 1.1

This is where we started

GETTING THE BOARD ON BOARD

After spending a considerable amount of time updating our technology infrastructure, we were ready to tackle the website. We completely reenvisioned the way we were going to approach the library's online presence. The library would no longer be limited to a building with books. We would be both a physical and digital portal to resources and entertainment. Furthermore, we would begin to measure our success by the total number of people we reached, not just those who visit our buildings. Our new website would put the library into the homes of our patrons.

This was a radical departure from previous notions about how the library should serve its patrons. Now we just needed to convince the board a new website would provide more opportunities for us to extend our reach and relevance within our community. We would need to explain how the site would benefit our patrons.

When presenting the vision to the board, I used the metaphor of tearing down the walls of the library. We needed the community to view us as more than a building with books. We had an opportunity to become an ever-present portal to services, information, and entertainment.

I used the example of a child working on a research paper at home and being able to easily access a wide range of research sources from the library immediately, without ever leaving the computer. I went on to explain how anyone with a library card could have access to the latest best-selling novels in digital format for free, in a matter of minutes, twenty-four hours a day, from any computer in the world. Rather than focusing on any of the technical aspects of designing the site, I focused on something they could more easily grasp and appreciate, the impact the new website could have on our patrons.

In 2009 this anecdotal approach helped our board understand and embrace the changes necessary for us to become what we believed was a viable twenty-first-century library.

When we went back to the board for another redesign of our site in 2013, our approach was more direct. Technology had advanced in a way that allowed us to incorporate our desktop and mobile presences into one responsive website that conformed appropriately to any device, as well as fix some of the things we wished we'd done differently in 2009. Since the board had seen the explosive growth of our digital library, they didn't need as much convincing as they did a few years earlier. Success begets success, and getting their approval for the site was quite easy.

DIGITAL REPRESENTATION OF THE ORGANIZATION

Once getting the board's blessing, it is time to start working on redesigning your web presence. An organization's website reflects the institution and should be designed and treated with the same thought and care that go into building a new branch or creating new services. The website is its own 24/7 branch, as well as a portal to information about services in your physical branches. It's just as important as, and in a digital age sometimes more important than, your physical sites. Patrons, consciously or subconsciously, judge an organization by its website. If the site looks like a reference librarian built it in 2003, it gives people the impression the organization is low-budget, low-quality, and there isn't a concern, or at least not an emphasis, on providing good service. Visiting an unappealing website is the equivalent of walking into a run-down, unkempt building.

An organization's website directly reflects on the organization—good or bad. Regardless of the quality of services provided, the initial impression people get from your website determines how they feel about your organization. You can actually drive potential patrons away before they learn how wonderful you are, simply by having a poorly designed website. If it isn't appealing to look at, if there's an overabundance of text on the home page, if the graphics aren't high quality, if there doesn't appear to be any structure, if the links are broken, if patrons can't intuitively find what they are looking for, all of these things are telling them the library doesn't understand, or worse, doesn't pride itself on delivering a quality experience to the people it serves.

CONTENT MANAGEMENT

Any library considering a new website should expect to have that website designed using a content management system, or CMS. Joomla, Word-Press, and Drupal are examples of popular content management systems. At CCJPL, we used Drupal for our 2009 and 2013 redesigns.

When websites are developed without using a CMS, they are far more difficult to maintain. Your staff shouldn't have to learn how to write computer code in order to add new content on the website. And you don't want to have to contact your web developer every time you need to add a photo.

A CMS makes ongoing maintenance of the library website much simpler. You don't need a web developer on staff to maintain your website. Anyone who can figure out how to use any modern Integrated Library System (ILS) can learn how to manage web content on a content management system.

So, before getting into any of the design decisions you'll be making for your new site, make sure that you choose a CMS platform to build on. While there are fans of Joomla, and WordPress has come a long way over the last several years, I'm partial to Drupal. My bias probably comes from familiarity, but I like the maintenance interface and think it provides the most robust environment for library sites.

THREE-CLICK RULE

One of the first choices we made in deciding how to design our new website was to adhere to the same strict three-click rule we had established for our first redesign; web visitors must be able to access any other page within three clicks or fewer anywhere they are in the site.

Libraries often design sites that require up to ten clicks or more in a linear manner, requiring patrons to dig deep into menus and through multiple pages for information, causing frustration. Patrons will often abandon searches for content, and ultimately abandon using the site altogether, simply because it's too hard to find what they are looking for. Barrier to entry is one of the biggest challenges libraries face. We have to simplify our interfaces. A site must have an intuitive structure if a library wants to retain visitors. Difficulty finding materials, too many clicks, or confusing directions drive patrons away from the site, rather than inviting them into it.

The three-click rule helps tear down barriers to entry, making digital information easier to find, and the site more intuitive to use and explore. The menu bar across the top of every page on the site helps an organization adhere to the three-click rule. The menu bar contains broad categories, with drop-down menus for each. When a patron mouses over "research" on the menu bar for instance, a drop-down menu appears with choices such as "homework help" and "databases." The menu bar makes access to information readily available directly from any page on the site, and eliminates the hassle of digging through page after page to find content.

SITE MAP

The site map is a page on the website that is basically an outline of all content on the site, laid out in the way the site is structured. A link to the site map should always be part of the main menu bar.

If patrons are having trouble finding content using the menu bar, the site map can help them quickly get a feel for how the site is structured and where they need to go to access the content.

AESTHETICS/LAYOUT

People scan websites in predictable patterns, and libraries should put their most popular content where patrons are most likely to see it first. An effective way to accomplish this is to design the home page and landing pages of the websites in an "F" pattern.

NOTE: Landing pages are the main pages of the major subcategories of the website, such as Adults, Teens, and Children. They differ from the many content pages on the site, which are primarily informational in nature.

Jakob Nielsen, called "the king of usability" (www.nngroup.com/people/jakob-nielsen), did an eye-tracking visualization study in which users viewed thousands of web pages.[1] He found that users first read in a horizontal movement, usually across the upper part of the page. That initial scan forms the top part of the F. This is where we placed the main menu bar and search box on our site.

Users then move down the left side of the page and read across in a second horizontal movement that is typically shorter and forms the lower bar of the F. In this area, we placed a slide show, promoting upcoming events and popular services at the library.

Then readers generally move vertically down the page at various rates of speed.[2] For this reason we placed links to our Adults, Teens, and Children landing pages down the left-hand side of the home page. (See figure 1.2.)

FIGURE 1.2

"F" pattern

To catch patrons' interest, a website must also be visually appealing with an appropriate mix of text and graphics in the right places. Great graphics and photos attract readers' eyes and break up text so the site is inviting, not intimidating. On the other hand, too many graphics and too little text can make the site seem overly simplistic.

Graphic, images, and photos should be intuitively informative and as "easy to read" as the text. Viewers should be able to see an image and immediately know what it represents. For instance, a photo of children reading is a good graphic to use as a link to the children's department, and a family tree is an intuitive representation of a genealogy page. Use photos and images to help tell the library's story visually.

The chosen color palette behaves as the background for the graphics on the website. Color unifies the site. Choose a pleasing palette and stick to it throughout. We use a combination of blues on all our pages, with the exception of Teens and Children. For those areas, we used age-appropriate colors and graphics to appeal to our younger patrons. Though the colors used in these areas differ from those on the rest of the site, they are still consistent throughout their respective areas.

Fonts, like graphics and color, impact the way a user feels while viewing the library's website. The library should use simple fonts and keep them consistent. Fonts deliver messages. They are not the message and should not impede the message. Some fonts are much easier to read than others. We suggest fonts such as Helvetica, Century Gothic, or Arial for simplicity. No Comic Sans!

SLIDE SHOW

Slide shows provide a way for the library to promote upcoming events and popular services to every visitor. The slide show is one of the most valuable components of the home page and departmental landing pages.

Visuals should dominate slide shows, with more graphics than text. Ensure images are engaging, because the appeal of the slide show increases the appeal of the service or event being promoted.

The graphics on a slide should reflect the nature of the event or service, such as an image of a smartphone and digital-style text to promote a text-a-librarian service. (See figure 1.3.)

Update slides on a regular basis. With constantly updated slides promoting new events and services, the slide show is a great opportunity to make patrons aware of how much the library has going on.

I suggest randomizing the order in which slides appear, so each visit to the site affords an opportunity for exposure to a new service or event in the library. Starting the show on the same slide every time would limit patron exposure to later slides, because they're likely to find the content they're looking for and click away from the page before the later slides appear. Randomizing the order of appearance also helps make the slide show seem new every time a patron visits the site.

The homepage slide show should promote events and services universal throughout the library, such as downloadable e-books or events for the

FIGURE 1.3
Text a Librarian slide

whole family. Slides on department landing pages can be more specific to services provided in those areas. The Children's slides would be far different than those for the Adult area, for instance, because most young children aren't doing genealogy research, and adults generally don't read picture books. However, each landing page slide show should also include some slides with universal appeal, such as free downloadable music, because those services transcend subgroups.

Limit the number of slides in any slide show to eight or fewer. Having too many slides decreases the likelihood of individual slides being seen. Slides should promote only the library's newest, most popular, or most marketable services. Slide shows are a great way of showing patrons the library is more than a building with books in it, so make sure to take time to create quality slides that will entice patrons to click on them.

CATALOG

It's imperative that a catalog search feature be present on every page of the site. Most people visit the library's website to search for materials in the library's collection. You don't want to scare them off or frustrate them because they can't find the search box.

The header of every page is often the most appropriate place for a catalog search box. The header of the site is part of the top bar of the F pattern and the first part of the website patrons are likely to see. Since the header appears on every page, patrons can access the catalog search box regardless of where they are on the website.

A patron on the genealogy page might become curious about grave markers, for instance, and can immediately search library materials on grave markers through the catalog search right on the genealogy page without digging back through other pages.

For efficiency, we integrated both the catalog and website search tools into one box with a drop-down menu to switch between the two. Patrons may alternate searching for materials or through the website itself using the same search box.

When a patron performs a catalog search, make sure the search results page opens in a new browser tab. This way, they can search the catalog without being taken away from the page from which they launched their search.

As is virtually universal with modern ILSs, the search results page should include a link to the patron's account and ways to manage account activity. It's logical a patron may want to reserve materials from this page, as well as place holds, pay fines, and renew materials in one easy place. If your library's ILS doesn't provide a full suite of account management functionality, that is beyond the scope of this writing, but you might want to begin the search for a new ILS vendor.

QUALITY OF CONTENT

While appealing aesthetics, excellent fonts, a great layout, and the perfect color palette are the framework for a quality website, people visit websites for the content. Make every word and every image count. You've only got a small space in which to tell a big story.

Pair images with copy, and use only enough text so readers know what you're saying but don't lose interest or get impatient. This is not the place for long-winded explanations. Don't impede patrons' grasping your message by using too many words. Each word must "pull freight."

Always avoid library jargon and speak in laypersons' terms, particularly within menus and instructional areas. The copy on every page must be clear to everyone, concise, engaging, and error-free. Writing must be done at no higher than an eighth-grade level. A good way to accomplish this is to get a person or group not directly associated with the library to read and edit the copy so that it is understandable by a general audience.

Graphics and photos must also be easy to "read," high quality in composition and preparation, engaging, and able to tell a story, just like the text. Avoid clip art and low-resolution or uninteresting photography. They won't attract patrons and will make the library's site and the library itself look substandard.

Website content should provide clear information and tell a compelling story that encourages—not discourages—library use.

DIFFERENT THEMES FOR DEPARTMENTS

While the site should be aesthetically consistent in both overall color palette and layout, certain departments may choose additional designs and colors from the palette to differentiate them from the rest of the site. This can provide the opportunity to use color and design to appeal to different age groups in a more direct way than the theme of the overall site.

Teen pages, for instance, can receive design elements appealing to that age group, such as cool images, hip graphics, and language relatable to

FIGURE 1.4

CCJPL teen landing page

that age group. Teens are usually on the cutting edge of current trends and the design of the teen area of the website should reflect the library's understanding of that. Teens should feel like the library "gets" them. (See figure 1.4.)

Designs for children's pages should be inviting to young people, yet informative for parents. It's important to strike a balance. Don't cartoon it up too much, because parents are likely to be assisting their children on the site, and you don't want to repel them. At the same time you've got to use colors and graphics that grab children's attention. (See figure 1.5.)

Beyond themes specific to children and teens, the rest of the site should maintain the home page design, lest the site become a cacophony of color and style without a consistency necessary to provide a uniform viewing experience. Design changes in unexpected places are visually jarring, and the site becomes difficult to use when every new page looks different than the last.

FIGURE 1.5
CCJPL children's landing page

DIGITAL SERVICES

A website should provide as many services as possible in a way that lets patrons use the library without requiring them to drive to our physical locations. The library's website is not only an information portal for events and services within our buildings, but also a vehicle to provide a robust online library experience for patrons.

This is what we mean when we say we're tearing down the walls of the library. It's no longer just a building with books in it. It's a service center, accessible anywhere an Internet connection is available. Patrons should feel the library is providing a full-spectrum experience within the website itself.

Digital services that should be provided on the site include access to research databases, downloadable e-books and audiobooks, free music, and anything else that can be offered without necessitating a visit to the physical location.

At the same time, don't limit digital content to services provided by vendors or content already in digital format. See what conventional media is available that could translate to digital offerings on the Web. Think about how you might deliver content in ways it's never been delivered before. For instance, at CCJPL, we have a popular tape-recorded story service, Happy Talk, that was previously delivered via telephone to one child at a time. Parents could call in for the weekly story and put their child on the phone to listen. The phone line served one caller at a time, and stories were rotated weekly. While it was hugely popular, the delivery method had obvious limitations.

To take advantage of technologies that could overcome these limitations, we converted more than 100 Happy Talk analog stories and songs into digital audio files and embedded a media player into the library website, providing access to all Happy Talk content twenty-four hours a day. No one gets a busy signal now. This also opened the entire collection to day care centers and preschools to play stories and songs to groups of children during story or nap times.

Patrons have limited time, and delivering library services in this way provides a total library experience without patrons ever having to actually come into any physical location.

CALENDAR

While it's important to provide digital content through the website and make resources available without necessitating a trip to the library, it's equally important to promote services and events provided at the library as well. An up-to-date calendar of events should be available on the home page and all department landing pages, though content may vary from page to page. A link to the calendar should also be present on the main menu so access to library events is available throughout the entire site.

The home page calendar shows all events for all library departments and is the site's universal calendar. Calendars on departmental pages should reflect upcoming events specific to those departments, such as an annual genealogy event for adults, storytimes for children, or a video gaming party for teens.

The events page should have a drill-down, or selection, mechanism so patrons can easily eliminate what they don't want to see and select only events specific to them for display. For instance, patrons should be able to choose events for adults, children, or teens, as well as view them by location, such as which branch or off-site location. This is particularly important if your library has multiple branches with differing events by location. It's imperative that design of the events page and the drill-down mechanism be intuitive to all users and not cumbersome. Letting users check boxes to select locations and departments for their search is an effective way to accomplish this.

Shifting from a traditional calendar look to something more linear also helps patrons better navigate the events calendar. Calendars on websites used to look like a monthly calendar, laid out with a box for each day. The challenge with that design is multiple events occurring on a single day convolute the online calendar and make it difficult to navigate and understand at a glance. As patrons transition from traditional desktop platforms to mobile devices, a list-style calendar has become the de facto approach to calendar design, as it renders well on smaller screens. (See figure 1.6.)

FIGURE 1.6

CCJPL events calendar page

Listed events should each have a link to a page specific to that event with additional information such as dates, times, and contact information, so patrons are well informed. This approach to calendar design is the most effective and convenient way to provide patrons with specific information about library events.

REGISTRATION

Many library events require registration so the library can determine anticipated attendance levels and staff accordingly. Online registration forms let patrons sign up for events without visiting a branch to complete a paper form. This helps the library attract more patrons since the process is made far easier. Patrons don't have to leave their couch to register.

Another advantage is that registration records become a database of patrons who participate in events, which the library can use for direct marketing.

Registration forms should have required fields such as name, telephone number, and e-mail address. All registration forms should include an opt-out box so patrons can choose not to receive messages from the library. But the box should always be opt-out, not opt-in, so the default is that patrons accept library communications about services and upcoming events.

At CCJPL, one of our required registration fields for teens is their cell phone number. As most teens now prefer text messages as a form of communication, this is a great way to remind them of the events for which they've registered, as well as provide the library an opportunity to inform them of upcoming teen events. Texting is an effective way to engage teens. Text messages create the feeling of a one-on-one connection between the teen and the library. Text feels more intimate than e-mail. Teens generally view text messages as more important than e-mail because they are accustomed to receiving text messages from valued sources, like friends or family. The text also allows teens to immediately and directly respond to the library and for us to answer their questions.

The online registration system also provides a plethora of statistics about program attendance that's preserved indefinitely in a digital format and available to be exported into spreadsheets for study. For instance, more than 1,000 children registered for our 2013 summer reading program. On our online registration form, we require information on the

FIGURE 1.7

CCJPL 2013 Summer Reading Club online registration

grade they are entering, their school, and if they are "readers" or are "read along." That information lets us staff accordingly based on ages and reading levels. Beyond that, it lets us see where we are strong and what schools we need to reach out to. It lets us know who we are engaging and where we need to focus more attention. We can track trends in attendance for stronger and weaker programs. We know at what age children begin our programs and when their attendance drops off. We can even track long-term trends on the age at which children transition to reading for themselves. (See figure 1.7.)

The information gathered through online registration is an invaluable tool for developing future programming, staffing based on trends, and using the information gathered to better communicate with library patrons.

CONCLUSION

The library's website is the core of its digital presence. It is the first impression many people will get of the library. It's the easiest, most convenient way to introduce people to the library. They don't have to go anywhere. All they have to do is log on.

The marketing strategies discussed in later chapters cover the importance of encouraging users to visit the library's website. When they get there, they need to find an easy-to-use, visually appealing site which shows that the library understands the value of its online presence and strives to provide a quality online experience for its patrons.

SUMMARY POINTS

- When seeking approval for a new website, avoid technical jargon. Use anecdotal examples to show the value a new website can bring to the community.
- The library's website is a reflection of the library itself. Treat it accordingly.
- Adhere to the three-click rule for easy navigation of the site.
- A menu bar with drop-down menus across the top of every page makes navigation quick and easy.
- The site map is an easy-to-use outline of the website and should be included on the main menu.
- Consider using the F pattern layout to take advantage of how users view websites.
- Strike a balance between text and images.
- Use only high-quality, easy-to-read, and relevant images.
- Carefully choose a color palette and stick to it.
- Select simple fonts that don't impede your message.
- Slide shows deliver important news up-front for every visitor.
- Update slide shows often, so content remains fresh.
- Promote library-wide services on the home page slide show and those with a narrower focus on departmental pages.
- The catalog search must be present on every page of the site and is best placed in the page header. Don't make patrons search for it.
- Consider integrating the catalog and site searches in one box with a drop-down menu for patron convenience.
- Catalog search results should open in a new tab so patrons may quickly return to their original page.
- Patrons visit websites mainly for content. Make content easy to access and understand.

- Make every word and image count. You've got a small space in which to tell a big story.
- Speak in laypersons' terms. Avoid library jargon.
- Graphics and photos must be easy to read and tell a story.
- Keep the site aesthetically consistent in palette and layout but allow departments to differentiate themselves and appeal directly to their audiences.
- Provide events calendars on the home page and all department landing pages.
- Include a link to events in the main menu bar.
- Include an easy-to-use drill-down function on the events page so patrons can sort through events and find the ones of interest to them.
- Use a list-style calendar, rather than a box-type monthly calendar.
- Events on the calendar should link to a page with information specific to the event.
- Online registration lets the library anticipate event participation and staff accordingly.
- Registration information becomes a database of patrons for direct marketing.
- Allow patrons to opt out, not in, of direct marketing.
- Information collected through online registration forms may be stored and studied to predict needs and evaluate program effectiveness.

NOTES

1. "Nielsen Norman Group," Jakob Nielsen, Ph.D. and principal at Nielsen Norman Group, n.d.

2. Jakob Nielsen, Nielsen Norman Group, "F-Shaped Pattern for Reading Web Content," April 17, 2006, www.nngroup.com/articles/f-shaped-pattern-reading-web-content.

2

GOING MOBILE

WITH ITS RELEASE in 2007, the iPhone spurred a mobile revolution that has untethered web users from desktop computers and put the Internet into their hands, literally, everywhere they go. More than 50 percent of American adults now own smartphones. Smartphones are on pace to be the fastest-growing technological advance in the history of mankind. We've not seen technology grow so rapidly since the home television craze of the 1950s, which was long thought to be a technological leap that would never be surpassed.

Laptops are replacing desktops, tablets are replacing laptops, and smartphones are swiftly eclipsing all other web access devices.

When we at CCJPL started considering development of a mobile website in 2009, it was a relatively forward-thinking move in the earlier part of the mobile transition. Now it's a must for virtually any organization with a web presence. Given the number of our patrons accessing web content on mobile platforms, libraries have to have a mobile website.

Since tablets and smartphones render websites on smaller displays than desktop computers do, traditional websites don't conform well to mobile devices and are difficult to navigate. Desktop websites rendered on mobile devices present a frustrating barrier to entry to library resources for mobile users. These patrons simply won't visit your site if they're constantly having to pinch and zoom to navigate a desktop website on their mobile device. A mobile website renders correctly on the small screens of mobile devices. It keeps the user from having to adjust the size of the text or scroll around a desktop website to see all the content.

There are two types of mobile websites—stand-alone mobile sites and responsive sites. A stand-alone mobile website is developed independent of the library's main website and generally does not include access to all of the library resources available on the main site. A responsive website, by contrast, is a single website designed to "respond" to the device a patron is using and render correctly on any platform, whether it be desktop, tablet, or smartphone. The initial discussion in this chapter will be about building a stand-alone mobile site, for readers who are satisfied with their current library website and only want to extend their web presence to the mobile environment. At chapter's end, we'll discuss responsive web design for those interested in the most effective way to develop an entirely new web presence.

WEBSITE VS. APP

There are two main ways to provide mobile content, apps or mobile websites. I am of the opinion that mobile websites are far better suited to meet the needs of libraries and our patrons. Libraries are portals to information, entertainment, and resources. Your desktop website, likewise, is a digital portal to information, entertainment, and resources. Your mobile website serves the same purpose, just on a smaller screen. Apps, on the other hand, are self-contained programs that perform a function, such as games or accounting software. The following considerations led to our decision to build a mobile website rather than an app for our mobile presence at CCJPL.

DRAWBACKS OF APPS

- There are multiple operating systems in the mobile environment. In order to reach the widest audience, every app has to be developed for at least two operating systems, Apple's iOS for iPhones and iPads, and Android for those devices using Google's operating system.
- Just like the software for PCs vs. Macs, software for each mobile operating system is coded differently and app developers must code each independently. Applications designed for iPhone will not function correctly on Android, and vice versa. The developer must understand how to write software for both.
- There are two primary app stores, one for Apple devices and another for Android-based devices. Once your apps are ready,

you must list them in the stores. Patrons must know the name of the app so they can search for it and install it on their device. It is difficult to post direct links to the apps on your marketing material. So the app isn't conveniently accessible without requiring the patron to search the app store, download the app, and install it. This requires extra, sometimes confusing, steps before patrons can access your services.

- Patrons must update their mobile library app every time the library adds content or there is a change in the operating system. Without updating, patrons miss out on new offerings or their app may stop working completely.
- App development and maintenance for multiple platforms can be extremely costly.

ADVANTAGES OF MOBILE WEBSITES

- Mobile sites automatically render appropriately on any mobile device, regardless of screen size.
- All mobile devices have a factory-installed web browser, which is the only application required to access a mobile site.
- The mobile site is platform-independent, and all coding is done on the site itself; therefore developers don't need to upload anything to an app store.
- Patrons don't have to download anything to use the site. All they need to know is a web address.
- It's easy to promote the library's mobile presence by including hyperlinks on social media or in e-mails, which will take patrons directly to the mobile site.
- Patrons can find the site quickly and easily using a search engine. Since code can be written on the library's main site to detect mobile devices, one web address can direct patrons to the correct site, whether they are using a mobile device or PC.
- All information is immediately available without users having to update anything, ever. So if you add a new feature to the website, the next time the user pulls up the site, they'll have access to it.
- All the work takes place on our end and is seamless and effortless for patrons.

Mobile websites are more cost-effective, present a lower barrier to entry for patrons, and provide the most current library information. They simply meet the library's needs better than apps. With that being said, we still incorporate app access within our mobile website. We have links to our OverDrive catalog and Freegal music, both of which have apps. Apps aren't bad things. They just serve specific purposes. OverDrive's app is an e-reader and audiobook player. The Freegal app is an MP3 music player. The library's mobile website is a portal to these and many other services.

CONVINCING THE BOARD

We approached the board about the development of a mobile website just under a year after launching the new main library website. It was late 2010, and we wanted our patrons to have access to the library everywhere they went, whether hiking in the park or lounging at the beach—anywhere they'd take a mobile device.

Excited about the opportunities a mobile presence would provide the library, I explained to the board that we were in the early stages of a mobile revolution. Rarely have libraries been in a position to participate in such a dynamic shift in the consumption of information. Libraries are normally challenged with trying to catch up to established technologies. A mobile site, I told them, would let us be at the forefront of the transition to mobile and already present in the space as our patrons migrated to mobile platforms.

Board members are generally dedicated to their communities and committed to the library and its services, but they're not necessarily technology experts. For this reason, it's important to talk to the board within a framework they can understand. Explain the advantages technologies can provide to patrons, rather than the technologies themselves. I told our board the story of a library in your pocket, to illustrate the advantages of a mobile library. I explained how a mobile library lets a patron in a bookstore pull their smartphone from their pocket and check the library's collection for the material they're considering purchasing. They can place a hold on the material and come to the library to pick it up. Or they can download the title digitally, as an e-book or audiobook, and begin reading or listening to it while still standing in the bookstore. The whole library was available in their pocket, along with the money they saved.

I also explained how cellular and ever-expanding Wi-Fi technologies would allow the library's mobile site to be virtually universally accessible. A person sunning on a Mediterranean beach, for example, could take out their smartphone, download an e-book from our library, and begin reading immediately, without ever pulling their toes out of the sand. We called it, "Your library, everywhere you are," and the board gave us their approval.

MOBILE LIBRARY

Having gotten board approval and determined a mobile website, not an app, was the best for the library, we had to determine which library resources patrons would want to access on mobile devices, and which ones would need to remain desktop-exclusive. We eventually decided that we'd provide the following services to mobile patrons:

- Access library branch locations and hours
- Text a librarian
- Download e-books, audiobooks, and free music
- Access information about library events
- Learn when children's story times or other children's activities are scheduled
- Check the availability of materials through the library catalog
- Manage their library account, place holds, and renew materials
- Access database research information
- Access library social media accounts, such as Facebook, YouTube, or Twitter

After determining what content we would provide, we turned our attention to design and aesthetics for the mobile site. Just as we had done on the main website, we chose images and text for the mobile site that were relevant and recognizable to laypeople. On the home page, the links consisted of a series of small icons with text descriptions to the right, each representing different content on the site. Due to the small screens on mobile devices, the icons had to be immediately recognizable and easy to understand. We included the banner image and color palette from the desktop website, to maintain continuity across platforms. (See figure 2.1.)

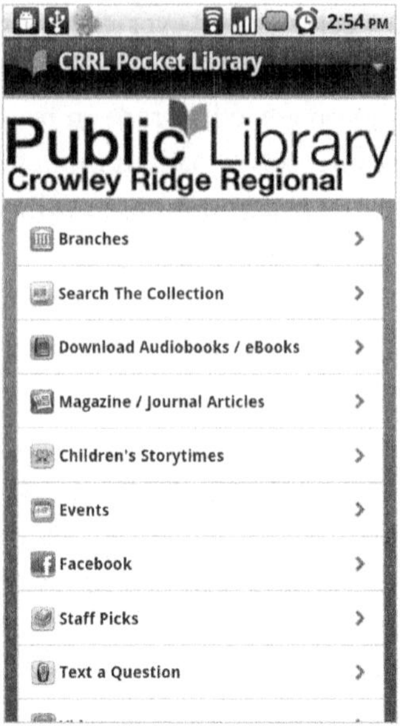

FIGURE 2.1

Home screen of our first mobile site

The site was designed using a heavily modified WordPress template. WordPress was originally designed as a blogging platform, but has since grown into a fully functional platform for the development of virtually any type of website. Using the WordPress template provided significant functionality with relatively low development costs, as there were a number of features already built into the template that we could take advantage of, and our developers had experience building mobile sites in Wordpress. One of the biggest advantages of designing in WordPress was that the template we chose came with a drop-down menu bar across the top. It drops down when tapped and provides access to any location on the site from any other location on the site. This allowed us to adhere to the three-click rule, even in the mobile environment.

Designing a mobile website differs from designing a desktop site. Libraries can take advantage of features mobile devices offer that are not available on desktop computers. You can integrate these features to provide greater convenience for your patrons. For instance, the library address can be linked to the mapping applications on smartphones, allowing patrons to access maps and driving directions with a single tap. Branch phone numbers can be configured to launch the phone dialer, and e-mail addresses can be tapped to send an e-mail to the library. Even a text-a-librarian service can be configured so that tapping that number brings up the phone's text messenger. Taking advantage of these functionalities creates a more robust and seamless experience for the user.

MOBILE FEATURES

Knowing what services we wanted to provide our patrons in a mobile environment, we created the following links on the home page of our mobile site. The access provided in the mobile environment may differ from library to library, but these links should be a good starting point for most libraries. Keep in mind that the front page of your library's mobile site should be clean and easy to navigate, so don't overwhelm patrons with too many options.

CATALOG

One of the primary reasons any patron accesses the library website on any platform is to search the catalog for available materials. The catalog is the most crucial component of the library's mobile presence. Mobile access to the catalog provides patrons with anytime, anywhere access to the library's entire collection, as well as account management functions such as placing holds or renewing titles.

We purchased AirPAC, Innovative Interfaces mobile catalog, which integrates directly with the catalog used on desktop computers. Most ILS systems offer a mobile version of their catalog. It is imperative that the catalog used on the library's mobile site is the mobile version of the catalog. The desktop version of the catalog is far too cumbersome to navigate on a small screen.

E-BOOKS AND AUDIOBOOKS

We offer e-books and audiobooks at CCJPL through OverDrive. OverDrive provides a mobile platform for easy access to the library's digital titles, just as AirPAC provides access to the entirety of the library's physical collection. With the installation of the OverDrive app, patrons can quickly and easily download e-books and audiobooks to their mobile device from anywhere in the world, any time, and have instant access to the material. Providing access to OverDrive in a mobile environment creates a simpler, more seamless user experience than having to download digital titles to a computer and then transferring them to a mobile device.

FREE MUSIC

We subscribe to LibraryIdea's Freegal music. Freegal's catalog includes over two million songs from Sony Music and a number of independent record labels. Freegal's mobile app lets patrons download a predetermined number of songs, generally three, each week from the library for free. The library pays an annual subscription for this service. Patrons own the music they download and can keep it forever.

When a patron taps the Freegal link, coding on the library's mobile website determines the operating system of the patron's mobile device. The patron is then directed to the download page of the Freegal app in the appropriate app store. From there, they can simply install the app and start downloading music.

Once patrons have downloaded music through Freegal, they can transfer it to any other device they want to use, whether it's the laptop in their office, the MP3 stereo in their kitchen, or the smartphone they use while working out at the gym.

LIBRARIES AND HOURS

Patrons need easy access to information about their local library branch, such as the hours of operation, the street address, and the phone number for contacting the location. Tapping the Libraries and Hours icon on the library's mobile website home screen takes users to a landing page where they get a list of all branch locations within the library system. Selecting one of the branches brings up an information page about that branch.

The branch pages each include basic information about the library, a picture of the location, and hours of operation so patrons can tell at a glance when the branch is open. Beyond providing basic information, the branch information page is an area where libraries can take advantage of some of the integrated functions of smartphones. If you include the branch librarian's e-mail address, patrons can tap it and send an e-mail right to a librarian. The address for the physical location can be tapped to bring up a map or navigation tool with turn-by-turn directions from the patron's present location to the library. And the telephone number displayed on the page can be tapped, allowing the patron to call the branch without having to remember the phone number or switch back and forth between the library site and

FIGURE 2.2

Caraway branch page from our first mobile site

their phone's dialer. The integration of these sorts of functions provides a sense of overall polish and completeness to your website, as well as easy access to the library for patrons. (See figure 2.2.)

ONLINE RESEARCH

While most database providers have yet to develop convenient mobile access to their materials, EBSCO has developed an easy-to-use mobile version of its database collection. Patrons can access citable sources for research or search a wide range of magazine articles directly from their mobile devices. Though it isn't the most convenient method of doing research, the addition of the resource was easy to implement and has some value in providing anywhere, anytime access to EBSCO's offerings.

As the number of databases increases in the mobile environment, libraries should consider creating a landing page with a list of available databases. This way, there's still only one research link taking up real estate on the home page and it can take visitors to the landing page, allowing them to choose the resource best suited for their needs.

EVENT CALENDAR

We discussed the design of the library's calendar layout in the previous chapter, specifically the listing of events in a single column. The single-column layout allows patrons on mobile devices to easily scroll through events by date, and is starting to replace the thirty-day calendar layout on all platforms as a result. Our current, responsive site uses the same calendar for all platforms. However, when we developed our stand-alone mobile site, we had to incorporate information from the thirty-day calendar on our main site into a mobile-friendly, single-column format.

The person managing the calendar of events for the library should have to enter the information only once and have it automatically populate to both the desktop and mobile sites. For our stand-alone mobile site, we accomplished this through coding within the calendar on the main site. Each time the calendar on the main library website was updated, the updates were automatically pushed to the calendar on the mobile site. For the person managing the events, as well as patrons, this process was seamless.

Tapping on any event should take a user to a page specific to that event, rendered in a mobile format and providing the same information that would be available on the desktop site.

Mobile registration forms may also be integrated into the events calendar for patrons to register for events while on the go, just as they could on their home computers.

TEXT-A-LIBRARIAN

The link to our text-a-librarian phone number launches the text messenger on a patron's smartphone and lets them text a question to the staff. We built our text-a-librarian service around Google Voice, allowing patrons to text questions to the library and staff to respond to those questions via the Google Voice web interface. It's a pretty simple process, as the tab for Google Voice stays open at all times on the computers at the reference desk, so staff can see when new texts arrive. Whether writing a research paper, settling a bet, or trying to sound smart at a party, patrons can find out just about anything they want to know within minutes, whether it's who won the 1947 World Series or if *The Hunger Games* is a nonfiction title.

SOCIAL MEDIA ACCESS

Make it easy for patrons to find you on social media. Tapping the social media icon on the main page of our mobile website takes users to a landing page listing the social media platforms on which the library engages. Links to social media platforms from this page should point directly to the library's Facebook page, its YouTube channel, its Twitter account, and so on. By linking directly to the library's social media presences, you make it easy for patrons to like, follow, or subscribe to the library's social media accounts. Printed materials can encourage patrons to follow the library on social media, but the library's mobile site makes it as simple as tapping an icon on your phone.

CHILDREN'S STORY TIMES

At least at our library, there are so many children's events going on that parents can have trouble keeping track of them all. Story-time schedules vary by age group and change seasonally at our library and this can get confusing. By linking to the story-time schedule on the library's mobile home page, you can provide parents with quick, convenient access to the library's regularly scheduled activities for kids.

READING SUGGESTIONS

Some patrons appreciate having staff suggest titles they've enjoyed or that are popular. If your library creates a page for reading suggestions, update your suggestions page often so patrons find fresh content and new ideas. It's also a good idea to have staff recommend books from varying genres so that you have something that appeals to a wider range of readers. Link titles to the mobile catalog so they can place holds on physical materials. Or, in the case of e-books or audiobooks, link to OverDrive, so patrons can begin reading or listening immediately.

RESPONSIVE DESIGN

The previous discussions in this chapter have assumed that a library has a satisfactory full desktop site and is looking to also develop a mobile presence to extend its reach beyond the desktop. I've been describing the development of a site separate from the main site that is exclusively for mobile use. But today's technologies offer a sleeker alternative. In 2013 we completely overhauled our web presence to take advantage of advancements in website development and developing a responsive website.

For those libraries also wanting to redesign their entire web presence, the most effective way to do this is to work with a web developer to create a single website with a responsive design. A responsively designed site adapts to any device a patron uses to access it, rendering appropriately on any screen size, be it desktop/laptop, tablet, or smartphone. This type of design allows for maximum access to the library's digital resources, as it provides full functionality and complete access across all platforms. In simplest terms, a responsive website shifts and resizes web page content based on the screen resolution of the device on which it's being displayed. (See figures 2.3 and 2.4.)

FIGURE 2.3

CCJPL fully responsive desktop

As seen in the smartphone image below, the site can also be coded to display an "app experience" page as the home page for smartphones. "App experience" just means that the page looks like an app screen, rather than the home page of the website itself. This page can have all of the mobile-specific icons of a stand-alone mobile site, for quick and easy access to the most commonly used mobile features. The "app experience" page of a responsive site can also include a menu button, such as the one in the upper right corner of our site. This menu button, when tapped, reveals the full menu from the desktop site, providing access to all the content not already displayed as icons on the mobile screen. (See figure 2.5.)

I've heard different people in the library industry talk about designing for mobile first and not including anything in the desktop environment that isn't available in the mobile environment. I disagree with this proposition, as there are a number of library resources that are still most

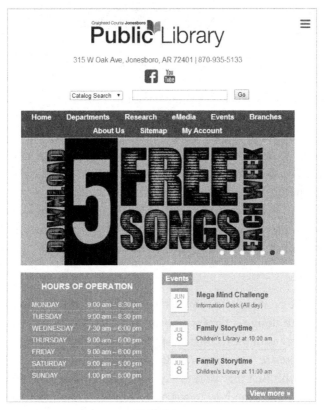

FIGURE 2.4

Tablet display

FIGURE 2.5

CCJPL app experience smartphone home page

conveniently accessed via a desktop or laptop. I can't imagine eliminating something like research databases from our collection because they aren't mobile-friendly. Providing a custom home page for smartphones is a better solution, in my opinion. This allows the library to design a full desktop website, but also customize the mobile experience for the user.

Just as mobile access to the Internet is the future of content consumption, responsive web design is the future (at least today) of web development. It seamlessly crosses all devices, providing a total user experience without limiting access to library content.

NOTE: The previous two chapters have included a lot of information on how to design a library website and mobile site, but I haven't discussed any of the technical aspects of how to actually build those sites. There are two reasons for this omission.

First, this isn't the space for teaching web development. The goal here is to teach you how to structure your site, not how to build it. Writing about web development would require multiple books, not just a couple of chapters in this one. The intention of these chapters is to teach you how to present your library's vast amount of information and resources to users in a manageable and unintimidating way.

The second reason, and I'm sure this won't go over well with some, is that I don't personally believe libraries, or at least the vast majority of libraries, should develop their own websites. The library's website is too important to leave in the hands of someone who isn't a professional web developer. Just because a guy in the IT Department created a website for a class assignment once doesn't mean they can *correctly* build a website for a library. I know some libraries have a professional web developer, or even a web development team, on staff. They are the exceptions. I strongly suggest that your library hire a web development company to build your site. Use the information in these chapters to help guide them through the process of delivering the site you want.

I know it can be intimidating for libraries to determine whether a web developer is good or not. Look at their portfolio of sites they've designed. Is it quality work? Have they taken on any projects the size of the library, or is their portfolio a collection of four- and five-page sites for local insurance agencies and accounting firms? Do they present themselves as a professional organization or is it a guy working out of his parents' basement? Anybody can call themselves a web developer. That doesn't necessarily mean they're good at it. And since we live in a digital age, you don't have to use a local company for web development. Professional web development companies design sites for companies and organizations all over the world. Choose wisely.

SUMMARY POINTS

- There are two main ways to provide mobile content, applications and mobile websites.
- For libraries, mobile websites are far preferable and easier to use than applications.
- Talk to your board in terms members understand and focus on the advantages of a mobile library for the patron, avoiding technology jargon.
- Ensure images and icons are immediately relevant and text is easy to understand.

- Mobile screens are smaller than desktop screens, and you must design accordingly, placing icons in rows, condensing your header and ensuring that text renders properly.
- Adhere to the three-click rule on your mobile site, just as on your desktop site.
- Library mobile sites should take advantage of the built-in capabilities that come with mobile devices, such as pop-up maps and driving directions, texting, e-mail, and instant phone dialing.
- Responsive design is the best way to deliver mobile services if the library is redesigning its entire web presence.
- A responsive site is one site that adapts to any mobile device.
- Work with a web designer to develop your responsive site.
- Responsive sites cost more initially, but the difference is far less than it initially appears when you factor in the cost of separate mobile sites. And the product is far superior to the alternatives.

CROOKED VALLEY REGIONAL LIBRARY

HOLLYWOOD, ARKANSAS . . .

While we were still developing our digital presence, I began thinking about ways we could use technology not only to provide online services, but to promote the library as well. I'd been fascinated with the idea of comedy YouTube videos as a promotional tool and thought it'd be fun to create one for the library.

In June 2010 I approached Phyllis Burkett, our library director, with the idea of shooting a comedy mockumentary-style video series about a fictional library, Crooked Valley Regional Library. The idea was to use patrons and staff as characters in the series, and have episodes run three to five minutes, each telling some quirky story about the library.

One of the great things about working for Phyllis Burkett was her willingness to listen to new ideas. If you could convince her that an idea was good for the library, she would often let you run with it. One of the scary things about working with Phyllis was, if she let you run with an idea, she often wanted you to start running immediately.

Phyllis liked the idea and, in typical Phyllis fashion, told me to get started right away. She suggested I make the first video to promote Genealogy Night, our annual patron lock-in dedicated to genealogical research, which was coming up in two weeks.

Having never written a script or directed a video before, I expressed my concern with her time line. I had come to her office to share an idea, but I wasn't even completely committed to it myself, at that point. Phyllis, however, had made up her mind, and previous experience had taught me not to argue with her.

Besides, who's going to give up the opportunity to make comedy YouTube videos at work? So I went back to my office and set up a YouTube account for the library (www.youtube.com/publiclibrary1).

■ ■ ■

"THE LIBRARY": A YOUTUBE STORY

I went home that evening and sat down to a blank Word document. Consider my dilemma: I had to write my first script ever for the premiere episode of a web comedy series, and on top of that, I had to figure out how to make genealogy funny.

"The Library" Episode 1: Genealogy Night

I wound up writing a script about a flashback to our fictitious library's Genealogy Night from the previous year. Jake, a mischievous character played by Joe Box, had spiked the punch, resulting in drunken mayhem at the event.

Initially, we weren't completely forthcoming with the six patron volunteers we recruited for the video. They assumed they were coming to the library to make some sort of public service announcement-style video to promote Genealogy Night. I figured we had a better chance of getting them to go along with our actual script if I gave them the details once we'd already gotten them to the library.

There were some internal concerns about "promoting drunkenness" in the library, given that our library is located in a dry county. Those of us involved in the project didn't really think we were promoting drunkenness. It was just a funny way to promote an event, no more risqué than a prime-time sitcom.

Part of our goal in making a video series was to push boundaries and challenge the notion of how a library is supposed to "act." Our community was unaware of many of the services we offered, and we were looking for creative ways to get their attention.

Genealogy Night was released in July 2010 and was a huge success, garnering over 1,500 views in its first week. We were extremely pleased with the response given that we only had about 1,000 Facebook fans at the time of the video's release.

As expected, we did get complaints from a few patrons and staff regarding the use of alcohol and other questionable humor. Those concerns were far outweighed, however, by the positive feedback we got from people who thought the video was hilarious.

We knew, going into the video project, this type of humor wouldn't appeal to everyone. We didn't necessarily want it to. We were comfortable knowing the worst that could happen is we'd have to take the video down.

As it turned out, this never became an issue. In fact, the participants in the video had a blast and enjoyed the attention, while other patrons and staff asked if we'd be making more videos and if they could participate.

Genealogy Night had its highest attendance ever that year. We'd managed to engage our patrons, build morale, and promote the library in a fresh and entertaining way.

"The Library" Episode 2: Four-Letter Word

After the success of *Genealogy Night*, Joe and I started talking about what we might do for the next episode. I saw our series as a library version of the sitcom, *The Office*, so we were focusing on ways to show our patrons the humor found in day-to-day life in a library.

Ultimately, we decided to satirize the stereotypical idea of getting shushed in the library. We convinced Charlene Roberts, a longtime employee of the library, to play the patron known as the "shusher." The story follows her from one frustration to another, as she attempts to silence everyone in the library. The episode climaxes with Joe's character, Jake, throwing a bucket of water in the shusher's face in the middle of the library. It was such a great shot we included a slow-motion replay.

Since we weren't promoting anything specific about the library within the story of this episode, we humorously interrupted it multiple times with still images promoting library services, à la Monty Python.

"The Library" Episode 3: Lover Boy

Our third video, *Lover Boy*, was created specifically to promote a speed dating event at the library. We'd tried having the event twice the previous year and were unsuccessful both times. We were convinced it was a good idea, but that we hadn't promoted it enough. We wanted to do everything we could to make sure this year's program was well attended.

The video follows staff member Bobby Swan's slapstick character, Henry, who decides to participate in the speed dating event. Armed with inappropriate pickup lines, Henry suffers through a miserable evening of being repeatedly slapped as he angers every woman who sits down with him. Then, when all hope seems lost, he finds true love . . . with the shusher from Episode 2.

NOTE: Even though we promoted it heavily and the video garnered over 700 views prior to the event, speed dating still wasn't successful. It was attended by four little old ladies and one creepy guy. Deciding to leave the romance in the romance section of the stacks, we haven't offered speed dating at the library since.

"The Library" Episode 4: Zombie Preparedness

With Halloween 2010 approaching and zombie fever in full swing, several staff members suggested we do a zombie video for our next episode. *Zombie Preparedness* was our first video done strictly for fun, rather than to promote any specific service or event.

We wanted to present a unique zombie story, but knew we couldn't be too scary or gory. We had no intention of making a horror video. This was a comedy series; we just needed to find the right angle to tell a funny story about zombies.

Given that our library offers a wide variety of programs featuring guest speakers, we decided it would be amusing to have zombies brought into the library for one of our Lunch-'n'-Learn programs—the zombies were tranquilized with synthesized vampire squid blood before their arrival, of course.

Reflecting on some obscure past encounter with zombies, Joe's character, Jake, decides he needs to do something to keep the library safe. With sedated zombies, a 1980's-style montage, and a cheesy shoot-up at the end, we went for the completely absurd.

We were starting to realize we didn't have to promote specific programs or services in order to promote the library. Being a part of the public consciousness and creating promotional material strictly for the purpose of entertaining the public had value unto itself. We were building an image, and that image didn't always have to directly promote a library service.

"The Library" Episode 5: Good Librarian/Bad Librarian

By the time we were ready to work on our fifth video, Valerie Carroll had started working in our Information Services Department. She was entertained by our video series thus far, and after we worked together on the script for a skit for the library's employee training day, she began collaborating with me on script writing for the videos.

Good Librarian/Bad Librarian was a black-and-white, 1950's-style training video for the fictional Crooked Valley Regional Library. As the characters in the video react to various customer service situations, the "good" librarians are predictably helpful and respectable. The "bad" librarians, on the other hand, act in a range of hilariously inappropriate ways: stabbing books, smashing printers, beating up patrons, using book carts for jousting matches, and holding a dog for ransom.

We were just trying to be funny, but I've actually gotten e-mails from librarians asking me if they could use this video as part of their staff training, which is perfectly fine, by the way.

"The Library" Episode 6: Book Club

Joe had been telling me for some time that we should do a parody of the *Fight Club* movie trailer, and I kept ignoring him. He finally showed me College Humor's *Jane Austen's Fight Club*, and basically insisted that we do something like that for our next video.

I wrote several drafts of the script, and Valerie and I worked together on getting the humor and language pitch-perfect for our spoof trailer, *Book Club*. It was the story of Skyler Durden—our take on Brad Pitt's character, Tyler Durden, from the movie—and the underground Book Club she was running. The video was funky and overstylized, an effort to emulate the look and feel of the original film trailer.

And the message we sent about libraries was subtle, yet powerful. At one point, Skyler Durden says, "You were looking for a way to change your library," then holding up an iPad with our mobile website on the screen, "You got it." We were letting people know this wasn't the library they'd grown up with.

On another level, this video was our love letter to *Fight Club* author Chuck Palahniuk. We were both humbled and flattered when Palahniuk shared our video with his thousands of followers on Facebook and Twitter.

It's been our most popular of the series, and its success felt like a wonderful validation of the work we were doing. (See figure I.1.)

"The Library" Episode 7: 50-State Salute to Banned Book Week—Arkansas

Given our other responsibilities at work, we had intended to take a break from shooting videos. We were content with the attention *Book Club* had received and were ready to focus on other projects.

FIGURE I.1
"Book Club" YouTube video

Then came an e-mail from Jenny Levine, with ALA, requesting we create the Arkansas contribution to their 2012 YouTube video project, *50 State Salute to Banned Books Week* (www.youtube.com/bbwoif).

Anticipating that many entries would be recorded readings of banned books or discussions about censorship, we again looked for a unique approach to the project. I kept returning to the idea of considering banned books from the perspectives of the characters in those books. The script included four vignettes, each with a famous character approaching the library desk and requesting their own book, only to find out their book had been banned.

The first two vignettes were Information Services Supervisor Nathan Whitmire as Huckleberry Finn, and me as Lenny from *Of Mice and Men*. The third featured Valerie Carroll as Howard Stern, requesting *Private Parts* and then going on a bleeped-out tirade upon learning the book had been removed from the shelves.

Finally, Joe portrayed Jesus, who informs our unnamed staffer, played by Nechia Whittingham, that his Father has sent Him to pick up a copy of the Bible. The startled staffer informs Jesus that all religious materials have been removed from the library to avoid conflict, to which Jesus replies that His Father will not be pleased. The video concludes with the caption, "Censorship Affects Everyone."

We joked internally that we might have just created the first Banned Book video to ever get banned. Juxtaposing Howard Stern and Jesus Christ can be dicey. Nonetheless, we felt that approaching this serious topic with humor would help spread the message to more people. The wide range of characters delivered our message about the universal impact of censorship, and through humor, we tried to make that message more accessible.

"THE LIBRARY": CANCELED

Even though they are a lot of fun to make, we no longer consider our You-Tube series an integral part of our overall promotional efforts at the library. It requires a lot of time, effort, and resources to make each episode, and we get a better return on investment in other promotional areas.

That's not to say we won't make another one if the right idea comes along and time permits. It's just that making YouTube videos has become more of a way to build teamwork and morale among staff, as well as have fun and celebrate the library with patrons; and less of a way to promote the library. It's hard to get people to slow down long enough while surfing the Internet to watch a video, unless it's put out by Miley Cyrus and 2 Chainz.

Though they aren't a focal point of our ongoing promotional efforts, these videos significantly shaped how aggressively we were willing to promote the library in other areas. They provided us with an invaluable learning experience about how to interact with our patrons.

They taught us the library didn't have to take itself so seriously. We could get away with being a little edgy. Our community liked the fact that its library had a sense of humor.

The things we learned from our YouTube experience have permeated virtually every other aspect of our library marketing strategy.

BIG SCREEN DEBUT

Don't let me give you the wrong impression. We didn't stop making videos. We just found a way to make them more useful. Back in the "Introduction," I mentioned that in 2009, Phyllis took advantage of a weak advertising market during the recession and purchased a thirty-second spot at the movie theater in Jonesboro.

At the time, we weren't even considering making videos. This was back when we'd just started working on the website and were using interns to do PR and graphic design work. However, as is common in advertising, the firm that provided the ad space at the theater was also willing to create the ad itself. All they needed from the library was a little information about the services we provided and a few photographs.

In October 2009, the library's first movie theater ad began running before every showing on all fifteen screens at the theater in Jonesboro. At the time, we thought we were pretty cool. After all, we were a library promoting itself at the movie theater, a marketing platform that reached a huge cross-section of our community.

We didn't think about what the ad actually was or how people would react to it. We were too focused on the fact that we had an ad, any ad, at the movie theater. The ad ran, unchanged, for four years. In hindsight, it was a matter of poor execution of a great idea. It was a slide show with some pleasant music and a voice-over, talking about all the wonderful services at your local public library. And it was boring.

CREATIVE WARFARE

By 2013, the creative team was in its second year of developing promotional material for the library. The movie theater advertising company had contacted us to let us know our contract was up for renewal. We'd all come to realize the movie theater ad wasn't reflective of the new, aggressive style we were taking with our marketing. We started brainstorming, trying to come up with an idea for a new theater ad.

And that's when we went to war. Well, not everyone. Most of the team stayed out of it. Specifically, Brandi Hodges and I went to war. She and I have the biggest, and truthfully, most overbearing personalities in the group. We are, in an almost comical way, opposite sides of the same coin.

My idea was to create a stop-motion video of an articulated wooden doll fighting a hoard of gummy bears while a list of library services scrolled up the right-hand side of the screen. My logic was pretty simple: it didn't matter what the audience was doing up until that point—eating their popcorn, talking to their date, playing with their phone, whatever. I was convinced that, when they heard, "Excuse me while I fight off this hoard of gummy bears," everyone would look up at the screen.

Brandi, while not having a video idea of her own yet, was adamant that whatever we came up with, it was not going to be a wooden doll chopping up gummy bears. She absolutely hated the idea, and felt, very strongly, that there were much better ways to tell people about the library. We had done a lot of crazy eCards and she had been a good sport, but this was where she drew the line.

It got pretty ugly, with neither of us willing to give in. Each of us went to David and Phyllis, trying to sell them on the merits of our position. To their credit, they stayed out of it, telling us it was our team and we had to work it out.

Eventually, I relented and abandoned the idea of creating the stop-motion video. I'd like to say I took the high road and was looking out for the best interests of the library. But the truth is, I'd done some testing and wasn't even sure I could make the damn thing.

NOTE: I didn't include this section to air our dirty laundry. But there are valuable lessons we learned through this process, about leadership and teamwork that I felt were worth pointing out. These projects are about more than just the mechanics of the process. There are people, opinions, feelings, and egos involved as well.

CATHARSIS

With some semblance of sanity returning to the creative team, we ultimately chose to tie the video to our 2013 annual theme, Art Typography. We decided to create a thirty-second video using an animation technique known as kinetic typography, which involves animating words as they move on and off the screen to voice-over narration.

Our first task as a team was to write the script. The name of our 2013 campaign was "WORDS," so we started building a script around the powerful impact words can have. In spite of the tumult of the previous few weeks, this turned out to be a wonderfully constructive and collaborative process.

It took us three weeks of scrutinizing every . . . single . . . word, but we eventually had a script everyone agreed on:

WORDS

They are hellos and goodbyes

Words define our voices

They are screamed and sung

They express our truths

Whether raising up, or tearing down

Words reveal our hearts

They uphold good and destroy evil

Words shape our world

Find the words to tell your story

At your local public library

Imagine. Create. Connect.

After finishing the script, we had to decide who would do the voice-over. Initially, we envisioned a deep, James Earl Jones or Morgan Freeman sort of voice. Unfortunately, they weren't available and we didn't have anyone in the library who sounded like that. But we did have Nina.

Nina Darley, who runs teen services at the library, had joined the creative team at the beginning of the year. She was born and raised in England and still spoke with a thick and unmistakably British accent. We were convinced the accent would get the attention of our Jonesboro, Arkansas, audience.

Next, Melloney Dunlap and I worked on the animation, her creating the text as graphics and me figuring out how to move them in sync with Nina's narration. It was a long and tedious process. I'm sure it can be done considerably faster, but I'm not an animator. I work in a library and was learning how to do it by watching YouTube tutorials.

In the end, it actually turned out quite well. Though, after four years of running a slide show at the theater and considering all the effort it had taken to come up with a replacement ad, I'm not sure of which we were more proud, the finished product, or the fact that we finished it. (See figure I.2.)

FIGURE I.2
"WORDS" movie theater ad

ABSOLUTELY FREE!!

For our 2014 annual promotional theme, we chose to parody Infomercials. David Eckert, who moved from assistant director to director when Phyllis retired in June 2013, had suggested the idea a number of times. He felt there was a lot of fun to be had with the overused, clichéd slogans and over-the-top sales pitches. He'd even suggested that we could have someone do a Billy Mays impersonation for the movie theater ad.

The creative team liked the campaign idea, particularly the movie theater ad. As far as we were concerned, there was no doubt about who should play the Billy Mays character.

David's personality was perfect for the role. He has a booming voice and a laugh you can hear all over the library. And you hear it a lot, because he's almost always in a good mood and laughing about something. If he hadn't become a librarian, it isn't hard to imagine him making a fortune selling cleaning products on TV. He has a powerful, positive energy about him all the time.

There was only one problem. Ever since I had convinced Phyllis to do a make-out scene with Bobby Swan in the *Genealogy Night* video, and then Joe and I decided it'd be funny to insert that clip into several subsequent videos as a joke, David swore he'd never be in a video, at all, for any reason, ever. I can't imagine why. After convincing him that it was a great way to introduce him as the new director, reminding him that the campaign was his idea, and promising repeatedly that I'd never do anything to embarrass him with any of the footage we shot, he agreed. And Library Dave was born.

We wrote a script promoting a library card as a solution to all the credit cards people used and the money they were spending. Brandi played the flustered, "There's gotta be a better way!" character, frantically shuffling through a stack of credit cards at a cash register. David was "Library Dave," our version of Billy Mays, standing behind a counter, bombastically naming all the wonderful uses of a library card.

After the requisite, "But wait, there's more!" and "And the cost? It's FREE! Absolutely FREE!" there wasn't a lot of time left to say much more. We threw in a, "Don't wait! Librarians are standing by!" at the end. Then it cut to the splash screen with our logo and website on it.

Wade Brightwell, circulation supervisor who joined the creative team at the beginning of 2014, did the voice-over for the splash screen, "This message brought to you by your local public library," and our branding message, "Imagine, Create, Connect," and we were ready to shoot.

Then we had to wait for David's beard to grow out so he could really sell the impression. Once David had a full beard, and his wife told us that he was shaving it by the end of the week whether we'd filmed or not, we shot the video. It was a really easy video to shoot and only required a few takes for each scene.

FIGURE I.3

"Infomercial" movie theater ad

Our new graphic designer, Micah Brightwell, and I worked on the editing and graphics. Within a week of finishing shooting, we were ready to send the video to the advertising company.

And that's what we've become . . . a library whose director is imitating Billy Mays in a commercial at the movie theater. (See figure I.3.)

In all seriousness, the video turned out great. It was funny, the parody was obvious, and it wasn't the type of advertisement people expect at the movie theater, or from their public library.

The movie theater ads, coupled with our billboards, have become the kickoff promotions for each year's marketing campaign. They are big, they're going to be seen by a lot of people, and they help tie all of our smaller promotional materials together.

And that's the story of what happened because Joe and I were bored one day and thought it would be fun to make YouTube videos.

GOOD FOR YOU: HOW DO WE DO IT AT OUR LIBRARY?

There is an extremely steep learning curve to creating videos. So steep, there wasn't even going to be a video chapter in this book until my editor insisted. I don't feel I'm capable of teaching people how to do everything well that needs to be done well in order to create videos. The most difficult part is editing, which requires an understanding of both computers and complex video editing software.

I don't "know" how to use the editing software. I mean, I know more now than I did when I started, but I couldn't get a job doing it. What I know how to do is watch YouTube tutorials, hours and hours of YouTube tutorials.

It's not very sexy. And it's difficult to actually teach people to watch YouTube videos. But it's true. Any time I want to figure out how to do something, like make a library card slide onto the screen, or words pop up in sync with Nina's narration, or edit Joe's 1980s montage, I look for a tutorial on YouTube. I've spent far, far more time watching tutorials than creating videos.

Directing, filming, sound, acting, script writing, all of these take research and practice as well. Regardless of the promotional opportunities, you have to decide whether your library has the time and resources necessary to learn how to create videos.

I don't want to make it sound impossible, however, because it isn't. We do it, and we're not all that different than other libraries. If you're a library interested in creating videos but unable or unwilling to invest the time and resources necessary to learn everything required in the process, there are some options. Libraries with local colleges might check with the film or media departments and see if any students are looking for internships or interested in creating the ads for free. Many students would consider it a great opportunity to get real-world experience and exposure for their work.

The same holds true for local freelance videographers who might want the exposure of a movie theater ad as part of their portfolio. Running an ad in the newspaper or on Facebook can be surprisingly successful in finding these sorts of professionals.

Regardless of the approach your library takes to create the ad, the most crucial part of the entire process is coming up with a creative idea. Your video should get the audience's attention and hopefully be memorable enough to make them think about the library, even after their film is over.

SO WHAT'S ALL THIS GOING TO COST?

It's difficult to measure exactly how many people come into the library as a direct result of seeing our ad at the movie theater. It's not like we can poll everyone who walks through the door. That'd be annoying.

So, instead, in situations like this, we try to take into account a few variables, and then consider the number of views the ad will get in relation to its cost. The variables include things like: environment—a movie theater; demographic reached—practically everyone in the community; attentiveness of audience—sitting in a dark room with nothing to do; media format—video; and immediacy of access to library resources (how quickly can they take advantage of what's just been promoted to them)— relatively low since their movie is about to start.

Other than the inability to immediately access resources at the time of promotion, which is difficult to achieve in most promotional situations, the movie theater would be considered a high-quality promotional environment. You're reaching virtually your entire community, have a captive audience, and are using a popular promotional medium.

Advertising prices vary from community to community, so it's impossible to know what it might cost in your community to run an ad at your movie theater. But, hypothetically speaking, let's say the average attendance at your local theater is 5,000 people per week. That's 260,000 people every year. If the ad costs $10,000 annually, the library is paying less than four cents per moviegoer to run the ad.

While that is more expensive than a newspaper ad, and certainly more than Facebook, we find value in the library having a presence in a place everyone associates with entertainment. There's still a certain "cool factor" to going to the movie and seeing your work on the big screen. We work hard to make sure the library's cool factor resonates with our community as well. Video gives us a unique way to do that, unique for libraries anyway.

As I mentioned above, it was never my intention to write this much about videos. Video is very time- and resource-intensive and creating quality content is difficult. That being said, I don't want to discourage anyone from creating them. But it should be pretty far down on the priority list, and definitely behind the other major initiatives discussed in this book.

On the other hand, if you feel you're the next Frances Ford Coppola, then by all means, grab a camera and start filming.

■ ■ ■

You may now return to your regularly scheduled chapter

3

FACEBOOK

AT CRAIGHEAD COUNTY Jonesboro Public Library, we started our Facebook page before other social media platforms, like Twitter, Instagram, Tumblr, and Pinterest, had become popular. Over time, we learned a lot about how Facebook worked and how to maximize our community exposure through our Facebook page.

At the time of this writing, we have almost 13,000 fans on Facebook. That's 19 percent of the approximately 68,000 active Facebook users within our service area. Facebook has become the primary means by which we keep the community informed about the events, programs, and services we offer every day at the library. It's also where we entertain patrons and give the library a personality.

COVER PHOTO AND PROFILE PICTURE

One of the first things a library must do when setting up a Facebook page is choose profile and cover images. The profile picture appears on every post the library makes, so I strongly suggest that the profile picture be a clean copy of the library's logo. The logo should fill the profile frame but not extend beyond it and appear clipped. Using the library's logo as the profile picture helps in branding and makes posts from the library instantly recognizable. Never change your profile picture. You want patrons to know who you are right away, every time.

The cover image located at the top of the library's Facebook page, on the other hand, is a large marketing space where you can showcase events and the library's personality. The library should change its cover image regularly. Your cover image is the first step in humanizing the library on

FIGURE 3.1
CCJPL "Air Guitar" cover photo

Facebook. It can be funny, serious, or touching. It's an opportunity for the library to present its personality to its audience. Choose photos or graphics that capture the attention of your visitors. This is a chance to have some fun, promote events, and entertain patrons. (See figure 3.1.)

NOTE: Though they are very lax in enforcing the guideline, Facebook technically limits the amount of text allowed on a cover image to only one-fifth of the image area. They have this policy to keep businesses from using the cover image as a digital billboard promoting $0.99 cheeseburgers in big bold letters and such. So, if you use the space to share information about an event, for instance, choose an image that tells the story and keep the time, date, and location information in one of the corners. If you use a good image, it'll catch people's eye, and they'll likely read the information as well.

ABOUT PAGE

The "About" page is probably the next thing libraries will want to complete when setting up a new Facebook page. It should contain fundamental information about the library such as the hours of operation, address, phone number, and the library's website address so patrons can access digital services.

The library's mission statement should be included on the "About" page to let patrons know how you view yourself and your work in the community. Include any information you deem pertinent about services you offer or anything else patrons may want to know. Although this is an information page, the library's personality should still come through in the tone in which the information is provided.

ADMINISTRATORS

Whoever creates the library's Facebook page will, by default, be a page administrator, but there needs to be more than one. Administrators are the people who have the authority to post content and manage the Facebook page. The library should designate a few employees as administrators so the library can post even when the primary administrator is unavailable. Multiple administrators also reflect different voices and personalities in the library and keep your page lively. You might select administrators from various departments so each can speak to his or her audience through the page. However, it is important for all administrators to understand the library's objectives on Facebook and to adhere to the library's rules.

The library should maintain a uniformity in its approach to posting, even while giving voice to various departments. Adult librarians may engage their audience differently than children's librarians do and use different language, for instance. But if the library's strategy limits text to three lines or fewer per post, which tends to increase the likelihood of posts being read, all administrators should stick to the rule regardless of their individual audiences.

You'll also want to use Facebook's activity log, located in the "Edit Page" drop-down menu, to ensure that multiple administrators don't overlap posts. Posts may be uploaded in advance and scheduled for later publication and the activity log will help administrators schedule posts accordingly.

All administrators should coordinate their posts through the log and see what others have scheduled and for what times. That way, a terrific post that's getting lots of engagement won't be obscured by another that comes too closely after it.

Making sure that administrators understand the library's posting strategies is critical to a successful Facebook page. It's important that they all understand what types of posts get the most engagement and how often the library has decided to post each day. Failing to do so will result in a Facebook page with little direction and likely cause patrons to "unlike" the page.

INSIGHTS

All page administrators have access to Facebook Insights, the tracking tool located in the Admin Panel at the top of the library's Facebook page. Displayed in easy-to-read graphs, Insights is basically a database that records everything relevant to the public's interactions with the library's Facebook page, such as the demographics of patrons liking, commenting, and sharing certain posts, or what hours patrons are most active. Insights is the behind-the-scenes monitoring tool used to analyze trends and adjust posting strategies. All Insights data can be exported for analysis or distribution to library managers. (See figure 3.2.)

Insights help the library understand how the community reacts to different types of posts. It gives you an opportunity to evaluate how status updates, photos, and videos compare to one another. Because of the pace at which people scroll through Facebook posts, visual posts generally get more interaction than posts that are text-only. Videos don't perform as well on Facebook as they used to, primarily due to the fact that people don't often want to slow down long enough to watch them. Virtually all of our posts include images now, whether we're sharing information

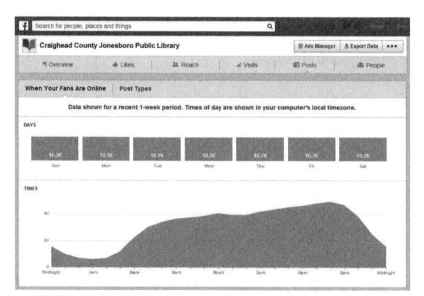

FIGURE 3.2

Insights can tell you when your fans are online here.

about events or services during the daytime or just being funny and entertaining our fans at night. Insights can show you which types of images perform best as well.

Analyzing your posting techniques allows you to adjust strategies to attract more interactions. At CCJPL, we learned that our largest demographic is women aged 24–55 who access our page in the evening. We've also, over time, determined what types of posts our various demographics prefer. We tailor our posts to maximize our visibility, targeting the demographics that provide the most engagement and scheduling posts for when those users are online. Use Insights to let your posting history help shape your posting future. This is your community telling you what they want from the library on Facebook.

BE HUMAN

You aren't connecting with folks in a business setting on Facebook. You are reaching patrons in their relaxed social environment. When posting on Facebook, you want to do it at a human level. You can't be an institution just providing information. You must appear casual; sharing resources, making people laugh, and engaging them in fun and insightful ways. The page and posts must give the institution a human voice. The library should talk *to* and *with* people on Facebook, not *at* them.

Facebook is a marketing tool for the library, and marketing is an emotional interaction. Delivering dry facts that sound like news releases is not effective in this medium. Your presentation should appear to the patron as if the library is part of their natural interaction on Facebook, just as their friends are, not something stilted or separate. Show that the library is part of the community and sharing with the community, not just delivering information to it.

Want to invite patrons to a library event? Speak to them as though you are encouraging a friend to join you. Let's say the library has a concert on the horizon. Avoid this approach: "The Beatles will perform at 7 p.m. Tuesday on the library lawn. Bring chairs. Refreshments are available. Admission is free." Try instead, "Hey, The Beatles are playing a free concert on our lawn at 7 p.m. on Tuesday. Don't miss it! And don't forget your lawn chairs and your appetite, because we'll have free ice cream too! See you there!" The personal approach is more inviting, generates excitement about your event, and builds connectedness between the library and the community. Make your post even better by including an eye-catching image of the band, or ice cream, or a group of kids dancing.

Your posts should also encourage dialogue with patrons, and you should always respond when patrons engage your posts. Show them you are a participant in the conversation so they'll know an engaged person is listening and responding, that the library is not just an entity that posts events on a bulletin board and walks away. Patrons want to talk with you, and they appreciate your answers.

Be personable but not too casual. A good linguistic tone to set is something just short of "business casual." Because you are trying to reach an entire community, be sure to always be inclusive in your approach and take care not to be offensive or discriminatory in any way. You want to ensure that all patrons feel welcome and included in all library activities.

HOW TO POST

- *Encourage Engagement:* Posting content that creates fan engagement is the key to Facebook success. Posts should make people want to like, comment on, and share them. Any engagement a Facebook fan has with your page also shows up to the fan's friends. The more engagement you garner with your page, the bigger your reach and the more likely others will "like" your page as well. One fan is not just one fan. Each is an exponential opportunity to reach more people in the community.
- *Keep Posts Short:* Social media are fast-paced. You will lose people's attention if your posts are too long. Keep your posts to three lines of text or fewer to avoid people losing interest before they finish, or not even reading at all because the post looks too long.
- *Post Pictures:* Even if you're just delivering a message about library services, an upcoming story time for instance, make the text something like "Hey, parents, bring the kiddos down to the library at 10 a.m. and share in our awesome story time." Pair the short text with a cute photo of a child and you'll get more interactions than if you're simply posting the date and time of an event. People don't share the fact that the library has a story time scheduled. But they do share really cute pictures of kids. And when they do, they share the fact that the library has a story time scheduled

FIGURE 3.3
CCJPL storytime facebook post

as well. People are naturally drawn to photos. Use that to your advantage. (See figure 3.3.)

- *Provide Links.* When promoting library services, remember to include links to the library website so patrons can quickly and easily get to resources, such as downloading e-books or free music. The links should take patrons directly to the page where they can use the service you are promoting. Make it as convenient as possible for them to use your services. Don't just send them to the website's home page and expect them to find it. The easier it is for them to access library resources, the more likely they are to return in the future.

- *Ask Questions.* One of the most effective ways to get reader engagement, specifically comments, is by asking questions. The questions can be serious, such as seeking input on what genres of books they'd like to see available for digital download, or they can be silly and issue an invitation for fun, such as, "Take the title of the last book you read and add 'with a chainsaw.' Post results." (See figure 3.4.)

These posts spur engagement and help humanize the library. They're an opportunity for the library to express its sense of humor. They show that you are part of the community and let patrons know you appreciate them and their feedback.

■ *Have Fun.* Facebook is a place to have lighthearted fun with members of the community. The library doesn't always have to be serious. Entertainment equals engagement, and engagement equals success. The more likes, comments, and shares you're getting, the more people are being exposed to the library. You're boosting your profile in the community and making the library a fun and entertaining part of your fans' Facebook experience. (See figure 3.5.)

FIGURE 3.4

With a chainsaw

FIGURE 3.5

Have fun with your community

EVENT PHOTOS

Always take lots of pictures at library events and post them on Facebook the next day. You are telling a story of the event with the photos. Post only your best eight to ten pictures of various scenes from the event. Too many pictures will dilute the value of the collection. Keep photos as diverse and as fun as possible. Try to include action photos with lots of people from the community. If Santa comes for a story time, for instance, don't post nine pictures of children on Santa's lap. Choose the best one of a child on his lap and also get photos of children watching him enter, reading a book, singing, dancing, or making crafts. It is important to make sure to let people know you're taking photos at your events and will be posting them on Facebook. Some people might not want to have their picture taken, so this will help them stay out of your frame.

These photos will make it obvious that people had a great time, and encourage those who missed the event to make sure they don't miss the next one. Photos express the emotions of an event far better than words. Encourage attendees to look for the photos they're in and tag themselves. Tagging people ensures the photos will show up on their Facebook time lines and in their friends' news feeds. This expands your reach and fosters a sense of inclusion among those who participated. Almost everyone likes to see a photo of their friends or family having fun.

It is important to post images that reflect the diversity of your community. The library is a place for everyone, and the pictures you post on your library's Facebook page should include people of all backgrounds.

These photos are also valuable for promoting future events, both online and in print. In the digital age, photos cost very little and can play a huge role in your marketing success. Make sure to keep all your library photos saved and backed up somewhere safe.

POST TWICE A DAY

Posting at the right times of day can really boost the success of your posts. Your patrons will often log onto Facebook in the morning when they get to work and are still drinking coffee, when they break around lunch time, and again at home in the evening.

Dedicate daytime posts to information about the library. Post events for the day at about 8–8:30 a.m. to catch people when they arrive at work and first log in. Yes, people goof off on social media before getting started with their work for the day. Some of those people will comment on or like your posts, and those interactions will likely generate enough engagement to keep the posts showing up on the news feeds of those coming into work about 9 a.m. If the library has an evening event on a particular day, you might consider scheduling the post around the lunch hour when fans are likely to check Facebook again. This will help to keep the event on their mind during the afternoon, and allow them to make plans to attend.

Avoid mid-morning and mid-afternoon posts, when people are working and less likely to be checking social media. Posting at 10:30 in the morning is practically the same as not posting at all, because there just aren't enough people on Facebook at the time to see and engage with the post. The person managing the daytime posts should schedule them in advance to ensure they show up at the appropriate time. Our library often schedules our daytime posts for the entire week. This decreases the opportunity for someone to get busy and miss the posting window for the day. If you do schedule posts, also make sure to monitor the posts and engage with patrons in the comment section. Don't just schedule posts and forget about them. Someone might ask a question in the comments, and the library needs to be there to respond.

One post per day should promote programs happening at the library that day. If you have a big event coming, you might want to post about it a day or so in advance and then again on the day of the event.

Posting in the daytime every day is important, even if you have no events or programs to promote. The library should be a consistent, daily part of your fan's Facebook experience. If there's nothing particular going on at the library on a particular day, promote services the library provides, like e-books or free music.

While the tone for daytime posts is factual and quick, the posts must be entertaining and move patrons to participate in your events. Facebook posts are short and can't include every detail about an event but should include a link to your website for full details if more information is needed.

Change your strategy in the evening, when people use social media to relax, laugh, and be entertained. I believe that evening posts should do one of two things: make fans laugh or tug at their heartstrings. This is the time to really reach out socially. At our library, our evening posts are almost exclusively funny or sweet images and don't always necessarily have anything to do with the library. These sorts of posts, especially the ones that wind up getting shared a lot, generate a tremendous amount of engagement and expose the library to a much wider audience than just our fan base. Every time someone shares a post, it appears on their time line for all their friends to see, fans of the library or not. We get an exponential return each time someone shares that goofy little cat picture. (See figure 3.6.)

NOTE: For me, the best example of how to manage a Facebook page is the actor, George Takei, of *Star Trek* fame. Takei's postings on Facebook are the master's approach to social media. He knows his audience and knows exactly how to engage them. You can visit his page at www.facebook.com/georgehtakei. If you want to be successful on Facebook, make the library's Facebook page the George Takei of your community.

FIGURE 3.6

Posts don't always have to relate to the library

Most libraries approach Facebook as a fact-sharing tool, but people don't generally use Facebook as an informational resource. No library will ever be successful on Facebook by simply sharing facts on its page. That's not what people want. Social media don't work that way. People log onto Facebook for fun, entertainment, and drama. Try to stay out of the drama. But the library can have fun and entertain people, which, when done well, results in sharing information about the library. Marketing is emotional engagement, not fact-based engagement, and libraries should use Facebook to engage the community at an emotional level.

THE ALGORITHM

An algorithm is a procedure for solving a mathematical problem. In the case of Facebook posts, the Facebook algorithm determines what posts show up on a person's news feed. A lot of posts are competing for people's attention and Facebook has to have a process of determining what shows up. Understanding how to take advantage of Facebook's algorithm gives the library a huge advantage when competing for space on our patrons' news feeds.

When determining whose posts to display, one of the factors in Facebook's algorithm is how many previous engagements an individual has had with a particular friend or page in the past. In essence, if you, as a Facebook user, interact with your friend Susie and like, comment on, and share her posts regularly, Facebook determines that you and Susie are close. Facebook will display Susie's content more often than that of, say, John, with whom you are friends but rarely interact.

The same holds true for pages you like, such as the library. If a person frequently engages with the library's content, Facebook will post more of the library's content on that person's news feed. The library establishes itself in the Facebook algorithm for that individual as something they want to regularly see. Facebook tailors the experience to the individual.

The library's post can still show up on the news feeds of fans who rarely interact with your page. Posts are given a value, based on, among other factors, the number of likes, comments, and shares the post has received. Each of these interactions increases the value of a post, with shares generating the most value.

Facebook's algorithm checks the value of each post the library makes and determines how many of the library's total fans should see the post, based on the level of engagement the post has received from other fans. So, if your post of a bunny napping near a book gets 3 likes, 2 comments, and no shares, Facebook determines people aren't that interested in it, and the post dies quickly, not to appear in other people's news feeds.

But if your picture of a cat reading *To Kill a Mockingbird* gets 200 likes, 150 shares, and 25 comments, Facebook determines this post is really popular with library fans and shows it in the news feeds of nearly everyone who likes the library, as they log into Facebook. (See figure 3.7.)

FIGURE 3.7
People like cat humor.

The amount of continued engagement determines how long the post will continue to show up on new people's news feeds. Posts with heavy engagement can appear on the feeds of people who initially log on up to 24–36 hours after the post first appeared.

We schedule our fun evening posts for 7:00 p.m. every night. Our target with these posts is 100 likes, 30 shares, and a total reach of 3,000 people. If our posts reach those numbers, they'll generally show up on people's news feeds throughout the entire evening and often into mid-morning the next day.

The goal is not to share facts. It's to keep the library on the minds of the people of your community. It's not that I have anything against sharing facts about the library. I champion the things we do every day. But we have to understand what kind of media works in what medium. Facebook's a place to let the community know that the library's fun or cool. This positive impression leads to curiosity. And when it does, they'll find the programs and services that best fit into their lives.

DROPBOX

All those funny images I've talked about thus far aren't necessarily original content that we created at the library. The vast majority of them aren't, in fact. Like most people on Facebook, we run across funny pictures all the time. But when you're looking for things that will really resonate with your community on a daily basis, it can get time-consuming cruising the Internet in search of funny or touching pictures to share with patrons.

Not many libraries approach Facebook the way CCJPL does. However, in the fall of 2012, I was fortunate to meet Jeannie Allen, marketing director at Kitsap Regional Library in Bremerton, Washington. She understood our strategy, and was using a very similar approach of her own. For some time, she and I carried on a friendly rivalry over whose Facebook posts would get the most engagement.

One evening in early 2013, Jeannie suggested we create a Dropbox folder to store and share images we thought would perform well on Facebook. Dropbox is a cloud storage service, a way to store, retrieve, and share files online (www.dropbox.com). We could save images in the Dropbox as we ran across them on the Internet and have them available for later.

I already had a Dropbox account and created a folder called "Library Facebook Images" to share with Jeannie. We began populating the folder with images we ran across on the Internet. Working ahead this way and sharing the images was saving us a tremendous amount of time, since we weren't scouring the Internet for content. We were creating our own library-related repository.

We realized this was a way to share our posting strategies and successful images with other libraries, saving them time and helping them get better results on Facebook as well. Both being members of the Facebook group, ALA Think Tank (www.facebook.com/groups/alathinktank), I posted on the group's page, inviting other libraries to join our Dropbox. In less than a week, we had shared the folder with more than 100 libraries and they began contributing content as well.

NOTE: ALA Think Tank is in no way affiliated with the American Library Association. It is an independent Facebook group of over 7,000 members (and growing very rapidly) from the library community, which grew from a handful of people who originally created the group to help coordinate shared housing at ALA (the real one this time) Annual Conference. It thrives on a lack of moderation and can get a bit "dramatic" at times. It's also populated with the most brilliant minds in our industry. If you provide questions about libraries, the members of ALA Think Tank provide answers. #partyhard

---

When speaking at state and national conferences, I promote the Dropbox as part of my discussions on Facebook marketing strategies for libraries. At the time of this writing, more than 600 libraries share the Dropbox, which now contains over 1,000 available images. Every member of the Dropbox has the ability to add content and invite new members.

Dropbox takes the guesswork out of providing content that will be compelling to your followers. It houses a host of high-engagement images to choose from for any occasion. If tied correctly to events or services you promote, the images will create greater interaction with those posts and share your message more effectively with your community. If you would like access to the Dropbox, e-mail me at ben@benbizzle.com, and I'll be more than happy to send you an invitation.

NOTE: Some people have expressed concern about copyright issues with sharing pictures found on the Internet. It's a legitimate concern. I think the answer lies in the nature of the images, the Internet, and social media.

When people create and post "meme" images on the Internet, they're usually doing so in the hopes that the images will be shared. That's basically why they created them. By the time we run across them, these sorts of images have likely been shared thousands, if not millions of times. There really isn't any ownership of them, or at least no way of determining it. The images sort of just belong to the Internet. They're part of the ecosystem.

There's also a fair use argument to be made.[1] As libraries, we aren't profiting from the use of these images in any way. We're using them to entertain our community and promote free library services. Nonetheless, if it were ever requested that we remove an image, we would do so immediately. They're just silly Internet pictures, and definitely nothing to fight over.

On the gray scale that is copyright law, I would confidently say that posting these sorts of images on your library's Facebook page falls into the very light gray area. No one's going to sue the public library for posting cat pictures.

CONCLUSION

The strategies laid out in this chapter work as long as libraries are willing to stop trying to push facts and information in a way that isn't engaging to viewers. As institutions, we have to commit ourselves to understanding what type of media works in what medium. We have to think more about what people in the community will react to than what we want to tell them. It's their news feed. Their interactions on Facebook will determine what they'll see. Engage your patrons in the ways they want to be engaged.

SUMMARY POINTS

- Use the library logo as the profile picture for the page.
- Change the cover photo periodically and use that space to market and humanize the library.
- Select several staff members as Facebook administrators to spread the work and expand the library's online personality.
- Maintain uniformity in posts and limit text to three lines or fewer.
- Use Insights to track which patrons are interacting with the page and what types of content are getting the most engagement.
- Be personable when posting on Facebook. Interact at a human level, not as an institution.

- Always take photos at library events and post them on Facebook the next day. Post only your best eight to ten pictures of various scenes from the event.
- Photos are also valuable for promoting future events, both online and in print.
- Include links in posts when promoting library events or services.
- Post twice daily.
- Post when your patrons are on Facebook, in the mornings around 8:00 a.m. and in the evenings around 7:00 p.m.
- Evening posts should make fans laugh or should tug at their heartstrings. Be playful and have fun with the community with evening posts.
- Take advantage of Facebook's algorithm. Doing so gives the library a huge advantage when competing for space on our patrons' news feeds.
- Be the George Takei of your community.
- Consider using Dropbox or another online image depository to share images in-house or with other libraries and ease your workload.

NOTE

1. "U.S. Copyright Office—Fair Use," *U.S. Copyright Office*, n.p., n.d., www.copyright .gov/fls/fl102.html.

4

FACEBOOK ADVERTISING

(or: How I Learned to Stop Worrying and Love Mark Zuckerberg)

JUST SHORT OF A MELTDOWN

It's May 25, 2014, Memorial Day weekend. Final edits to this manuscript were due to the publisher on April 15. I'm late because Facebook keeps changing its algorithm, which has, in turn, forced me to modify my recommended strategy for using Facebook as a tool to promote the library.

In fact, I had, at one point, deleted the entire previous chapter of this book, intending only to write about using Facebook as an advertising platform. In the end, I decided it's better to explain Facebook as a social engagement tool, as I hope to have done in chapter 3, and an advertising tool, as I hope to do here. It is both, and ultimately libraries should understand how to use it as both. I'm sure chapter 3 is grateful.

WHAT'S SO CONFUSING?

Ok, here's the problem . . .

One of the most challenging aspects of managing a Facebook page is growing its fan base. The posting strategies in chapter 3 work great. But what if no one is listening? You don't just start out with an audience when you start a Facebook page. You have to make people aware of the page, and then get them to like it.

There are conventional routes to gaining Facebook fans. The library's Facebook page should be listed on marketing materials such as bookmarks or postcards. Staff should be instructed to tell patrons about the library's Facebook page at checkout. The address to the page could be printed onto patrons' library receipts. Any number of ways may be employed to draw fans to your page.

But these strategies can be slow and tedious, primarily because they rely on the library asking patrons to remember to do something at a later time, rather than being able to take action right then. If a patron sees the library's Facebook page listed on their receipt, or if a librarian asks them to visit the page, we're depending on the patron, with everything else occurring in their life, to remember to find and like the library's Facebook page the next time they happen to be on Facebook.

Exacerbating the problem, the library is dependent on the consistency of staff in reminding patrons to like the Facebook page at the same time they may be trying to inform patrons of any number of other library programs and services.

These approaches will grow the audience of the library's Facebook page, but it will take a long time. And you don't have a long time.

SO WE RUN AN AD TO GET LIKES, RIGHT?

That used to be the solution.

For over three years, we ran an ad at CCJPL to gain likes for the library. I wrote articles and gave conference presentations, explaining how to create and manage ads to grow a library's following. The best way to use Facebook to reach your community was to use the posting strategies from chapter 3, while running an ad to gain page likes and continually grow the library's audience for those posts.

In August 2012, having developed an ad strategy for our library to quickly and inexpensively build a Facebook audience, I wanted to find out if the results could be universally replicated. So I decided to test the strategy.

I invited seven libraries from across the United States to participate in a study. I chose libraries that served a wide variety of population sizes and demographics, from Marshall County Public Library, serving a population of 25,000 in western Kentucky, to Chicago Public Library, serving a population of almost three million.

I requested that each library commit $10 a day, for 28 days, to run a Facebook ad, and allow me to manage the ad on their behalf in order to ensure uniformity among the libraries.

The seven libraries collectively gained 8,413 fans in 28 days between August and September 2012. Most continued to run their ads long after the trial ended, to this very day in some instances.

San Rafael Public Library in small San Rafael, California, had a Facebook following of just more than 500 before the study. They gained over 2,500 fans by running their ad over the course of the next year. Chicago Public Library joined the case study with 8,800 Facebook fans and has over 30,000 now, an increase of over 21,000 fans since the study began. Wake County Public Library in Raleigh, North Carolina, joined the study with a fan base of 2,200, which has grown to over 13,000.

With a successful strategy for managing a library's page and the ability to grow an audience through the use of a Facebook ad, libraries now had a cost-effective way to reach a significant portion of their community using the world's largest social media platform. This was pretty exciting stuff.

BUT . . .

This is the digital age, and things change.

That study was done two years ago. Those seven libraries gained a total of 8,413 page likes, for a total budget of $1,960. That works out to $0.23 per like. And that's a really good deal.

But what if you're starting out in 2014? What if only 1 or 2 percent of your service population are fans of the library on Facebook? Does it make sense to start spending money now to start building a following for your library's Facebook page?

In 2012 Facebook advertising was still viewed with a significant measure of skepticism, not just by libraries, but by the business community as a whole. But for those who had figured it out, Facebook was offering a heck of a deal. In the case of the libraries in the study, we could gain likes for our pages for an average of $0.23 each, and then could post content to those fans daily, at no additional cost.

It didn't take long for practically everyone in the business community to realize the value of running ads to build a Facebook following. With the influx of businesses and organizations looking to capitalize, the market got competitive and the price went up.

During the August 2012 study, CCJPL paid an average of $0.45 per page like. By January 2013, that had risen to $0.66. Over the next year, that cost slowly but steadily increased. In January 2014 we were paying $1.15 per page like.

That isn't nearly as good a value as it was two years ago. At the rate of $1.15 per like, it's going to take a lot more money for a library to build a following.

If you're just getting started and decide to run a $10/day ad to gain likes for your page, you'd be looking at spending $3,650 to have about 3,000 fans . . . a year from now.

3,000 FANS SOUNDS PRETTY GOOD

That's true. It isn't a bad start. But there's a problem here too. Not all of those fans are going to see your posts. In fact, only a very small percentage of them will.

Remember when I mentioned all of those businesses and organizations that drove the ad prices up, looking to build followings of their own? The second part of that strategy was to then post content regularly, in hopes of getting engagement. In some variation or another, they were all employing their own version of the Facebook strategy in chapter 3. That has led to considerably more content being produced. Everyone is jockeying for position on a very crowded news feed.

Facebook now has over a billion users and over fifty million pages. Where someone might have had 100 friends and been a fan of 8 or 10 pages two years ago, nowadays they may have 400 or 500 friends and be fans of hundreds of pages. There's no way for someone to see everything being posted by all the people, businesses, and organizations to which they connect on Facebook. The news feed would move too fast and it would look like Twitter.

The only way for Facebook to control the flow of the news feed and provide some semblance of order is to employ the algorithm discussed in the last chapter. Unfortunately, the explosive increase in content has forced Facebook to suppress more and more of it, thus significantly reducing the number of people who see any particular post from any particular source. Facebook pages have been hardest hit, as Facebook assumes people would rather see more content from their friends and family than they would from organizations and businesses.

If your library posts to Facebook relatively infrequently and only gets minimal engagement on each post, those posts are only going to reach 5 to 7 percent of your fans. You're only reaching a couple hundred of those fans with any given post.

If you post regularly, manage to get good engagement with your posts, and build up those connections with fans, you'll be able to push that number to between 10 and 12 percent.

CLEAR AS MUD

Ok, ok! Let's go back to those 3,000 fans we were talking about earlier. We'll assume that your library has run an ad for a year, spent $3,650, and acquired 3,000 fans. You diligently post twice daily, get pretty good engagement, and average 10 percent reach with each post.

For this example, we'll say each post gets the same level of engagement, whether it's an informative morning post or a funny evening post. That wouldn't actually be the case, as the evening posts get far more engagement. Nonetheless, this is probably already difficult enough to keep up with, so we'll just say the reach is evenly distributed. That winds up working out to 300 people seeing each post, or 600 people per day, since you're posting twice daily. Over the course of a year, that's 219,000 times that fans would see your posts.

That doesn't sound too bad, but let's take a look at how it actually breaks down in terms of delivering the library message to our community. First, we agreed that half of the posts were humorous or touching posts in the evenings. While we've discussed the value of remaining in the public consciousness, we did generously account for that value when we decided to attribute 50 percent of the reach to the morning posts, though they don't actually receive that level of exposure.

Given this concession, that would mean about 110,000 of your post exposures (the morning posts) actually informed people about the library. The library only has 3,000 fans, which means each of them is seeing, on average, 37 meaningful posts per year, or roughly three posts per month, for $3,650.

In the case of CCJPL, with a following of 13,000 fans, reaching each of them with an average of three posts each month about library services is pretty good exposure. But, given the current cost of gaining likes (and assuming that rate doesn't go up—which it will), your library would be looking at over four years and almost $15,000 to build that kind of following.

I have no idea what the world is going to look like in 2018. But I do know I can't endorse a social media strategy that's going to cost a library $15,000 to post cat pictures for the next four years. The strategy just doesn't work anymore.

YOU GOT ANYTHING GOOD TO SAY?

Actually, I do. I just needed to make sure everyone understood where we've come from and why old strategies don't always continue to work as the environment changes.

NOTE: Even though reach is dropping and the traditional route to gaining likes for your library's Facebook page is slow and tedious, I still believe it's important that libraries continue to maintain a social presence on Facebook. Other than the time and effort it takes to keep the page updated and remind patrons to like it, this does offer the library a free opportunity to promote itself, albeit to a limited audience. Keep in mind, those who see our daily posts are our biggest fans. We definitely want to put forth the effort to keep them informed.

But let's get to the new advertising strategy. This all came about because I was simultaneously preparing to rewrite this chapter (Facebook kept changing the user interface, making my instructions moot on three different occasions) and preparing a presentation for Demco. I was in the process of crunching some numbers when I realized the return on investment (ROI) just wasn't there anymore and I couldn't keep teaching the same ad strategy.

By pure happenstance, or maybe because we're almost always experimenting, we had just run a $50 "boosted post" ad promoting a Food4Fines event we were having during National Library Week. A boosted post is a type of ad where your library creates a Facebook post and then pays a certain amount of money for that post to show up on people's news feeds for a certain period of time.

Other than a few posters inside the library, we hadn't created any marketing material for the Food4Fines promotion. We had been concentrating on promoting our "Arts on the Lawn" event happening the same week. In a pinch, Brandi and I decided to see what kind of result we could get by just using a Facebook ad to inform people outside the library about Food4Fines. That's how our boosted post came to be. (See figures 4.1 and 4.2.)

FIGURE 4.1

Food4Fines Facebook ad

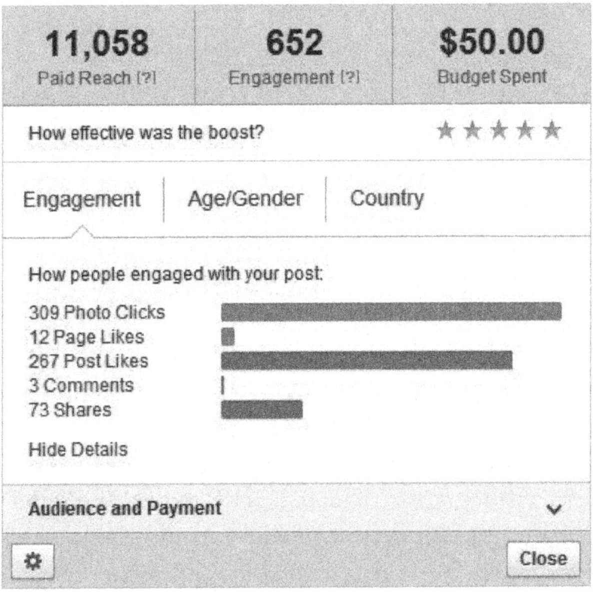

FIGURE 4.2

Food4Fines ad performance

As you can see, the ad received quite a bit of engagement on Facebook. Our $50 ad was seen by over 12,000 people. But the real measure of success would be how many people donated food items. Those numbers were even more impressive than the ad performance itself. Over the course of a week, we forgave $562 in fines and collected 725 food items (978 pounds). Some people donated out of goodwill, without any fines to forgive.

NOTE: At current rates, you can figure that a $50 ad will reach approximately 10,000 people. This can vary for a number of reasons, including demographics, major sporting events, holidays, and so on. But for our examples, we'll use this measure. Your mileage may vary.

ALSO NOTE: The $50 is just the example ad budget we're using. Your library can set any budget you feel is most effective for you. The numbers will all break down accordingly. A $25 ad will reach about 5,000 people, while a $100 ad will reach about 20,000. Libraries in smaller markets might not need to reach as many people as those in larger markets.

The success of our direct promotion of Food4Fines, coupled with the inefficiency of our old Facebook advertising strategy, got us to thinking of a new use for the money we'd been spending on Facebook. Rather than spending $70 every week ($10 a day) gaining fans, what if we spend $50 each week specifically promoting a particular program, service, or event offered by the library?

How many more people will download songs if we create an ad pointing them back to our Freegal page, and show that ad to 10,000 people over the course of a week? How many more people will show up for our summer concerts if we create an ad promoting them and show that ad to 10,000 people for three days prior to each show? What impact could $50 have on story times, teen programs, circulation, job services, e-book downloads, or any of the many other services we provide for our communities?

At $50 each week, we'd be spending $2,600 a year, a savings of $1,050 from the old strategy. And for that, we'd be getting over a half million opportunities to introduce library programs and services to not only our fans, but everyone in our community with a Facebook account, since ads reach people whether they're fans of the library or not.

Furthermore, this strategy can work, and work immediately, for other libraries as well. In the four years you'd spend building a following comparable to that of CCJPL, you can reach over two million people, promoting more than 200 different library offerings.

OK, THAT SOUNDS PRETTY COOL

Yeah, we were pretty excited about it, ourselves.

For our next ad, we were promoting a Skype session with an author. This time, instead of creating a boosted post, we created a $50 ad that would take users to a page we'd created on our website to promote the event. By doing that, we were able to highlight some of the books the author had written as well as provide more information about the event. We were also able to measure how much we were spending for each person interested enough in the event to click on the ad.

The ad appeared on news feeds just over 9,000 times, and was clicked 91 times, at a cost of $0.55 per click. Roughly 1 percent of those seeing the ad actually clicked on it. On Facebook, this is known as the click-through-rate, or CTR (number clicking/number seeing the ad).

NOTE: The $0.55 per click isn't in addition to the $50 spent to create the ad. It's just a reflection of how the $50 was distributed. $50/91clicks = $0.55 per click.

CTR and, by extension, cost-per-click (CPC . . . how much you paid for each click to your library website) can be good measures of the community's interest level in a particular program or service. If your ad is showing up on a lot of news feeds but getting very few clicks, as evidenced by a high cost-per-click, then perhaps people aren't that interested in the particular event or service. By contrast, if your ad is getting clicks frequently, then the cost-per-click will naturally be lower. This might be an indication of high interest in the program or service.

At the same time, these numbers may also simply mean you created a really bad, or really good, ad. There is an art to that as well, but we'll get to ad creation later.

We felt like the Skype session might be a pretty tough sell. Usually, author visits are heavily attended. But people like to meet authors, get their pictures made, and have their books signed. We weren't sure how many people would be interested in a web-based interview with an author where those other benefits weren't available. The relatively low level of interaction with the Facebook ad was indicating that there wasn't a tremendous amount of interest.

As it turned out, we had a total of nineteen attendees. By our standards, the event was not a success. This was, however, our first attempt at this type of program, as well as our first attempt at this type of Facebook ad. We haven't given up on the idea of author Skype sessions, as they're a great way for fans to meet writers. But we will work on some different approaches to our promotion of the events and see if we can garner higher attendance at future programs.

We were approaching summer, which meant we were in the process of putting together one of our biggest events of the year, our annual "Concerts on the Lawn" series. Every Tuesday night in June, we host a 6:30 concert on the lawn of the library.

Brandi had been busy booking bands, contacting sponsors, and running around in a bit of a panic for a few weeks. The creative team had settled on a poster idea to promote the series, and Micah had created the design. Things were falling into place.

The only real difference in our approach this year was, instead of running an ad in the newspaper promoting the concert series, Brandi and I decided we'd run an ad on Facebook instead. We were still doing all of our other promotions for the events. We put posters up around town and handed out fliers. We reminded patrons and posted to our fans on Facebook. Brandi went on the radio, and so forth. None of that changed from last year.

But the decision not to run a newspaper ad was significant. The newspaper has a readership of 20,000. In previous years, we'd been spending $250 for a newspaper ad to promote the concerts. Facebook has 68,000 users within our service area. With a $50 ad, we could reach 10,000 of them. The Facebook reach would be half that of the readership of the newspaper, but Facebook provided what we believed to be a better medium for the library.

Rather than a quarter-page ad on page sixteen of the newspaper, our ad would be showing up on newsfeeds and mobile devices. We simply felt more people would actually see it on Facebook than in the newspaper, even if we were only technically reaching half as many people. Besides, we were also only paying a fifth of the cost.

NOTE: This one is more like a soapbox . . . I find it odd that many libraries are completely comfortable with promoting events in the newspaper, but refuse to even consider doing so on Facebook. The medium shouldn't matter. We're just trying to get as many people as possible to use the library.

Like the Skype session ad, we created this ad to point users back to the "Concerts on the Lawn" event page on our website when they clicked on it. This would, again, allow us to provide additional information about the concerts, as well as increase exposure for the library's website. (See figure 4.3.)

FIGURE 4.3

2014 "Concerts on the Lawn" Facebook ad

The concert ad performed far better than the Skype ad had. Reaching over 11,000 people, it garnered 101 likes and 60 shares. It also received 332 website clicks, at a cost of $0.15 per click, with a CTR of 2.9 percent.

Obviously, we'd made an impact with this ad. There was no way a newspaper ad could get 332 people to go to our website. Facebook was not only providing better exposure for library events at a lower cost. It was also providing real-time access, something unavailable in virtually any other medium.

If ad performance was going to be a predictor of turnout, we were about to put the theory to the test. Lots of people had shown interest in the ad, but how many were going to show up?

Our first concert was on June 3. And no one showed up. No, I'm kidding. While we had an issue with the staff responsible for keeping count and didn't get an exact number, we had well over 400 people in attendance. By all accounts, it was one of our highest-attended concerts ever.

Not only that, but whereas we were only able to run one $250 newspaper ad to promote the entire series, we'll be able to run $50 ads for each concert this year, and still save $50 over running the newspaper ad. With four $50 ads, we'll wind up reaching roughly 40,000 people (double that of the newspaper ad) and point over 1,200 of them to the library's website.

OK, SHOW US HOW TO DO ALL THIS STUFF

You bet . . . and with pictures!

Since Facebook's entire business model is built around getting pages to run ads, they've made the process pretty easy. (See figure 4.4.)

After you've created your first ad, you'll have a new item on the left menu of your Facebook home screen, called "Ads Manager." From then on, you'll just click there to create and manage your ads. (See figure 4.5.)

We're going to create an ad to get clicks to our website, just like we did for our Skype and concert ads. This time, we're going to create an ad to promote free music and point them to our Freegal page. (See figure 4.6.)

Once you've chosen the web page, the process of creating the ad itself begins. The first thing you'll be asked to do is provide images for your ad. If you are able to do so, I encourage you to create your own images; that way they best reflect the message you are trying to convey.

FIGURE 4.4

Click on the "Menu" button in the lower right corner of the
cover photo and click "Create Ad"

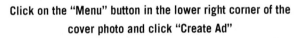

FIGURE 4.5

Facebook "Ads Manager" at left

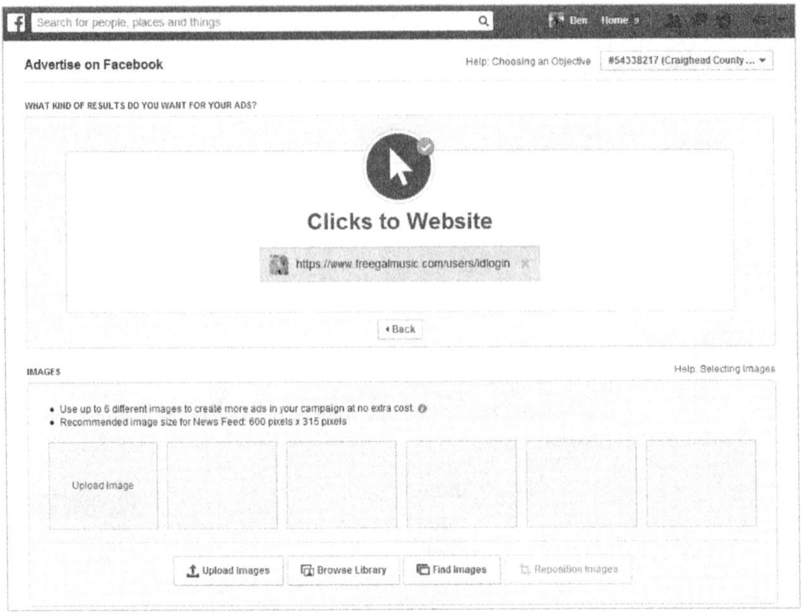

FIGURE 4.6

Paste the web page address into the blank.

The images you choose for your ad are very important. Remember, you're trying to attract people's attention in a very fast-paced environment. You want to create images that are going to get people to stop and click on them.

NOTE: The recommended size for an ad image is 600 pixels × 315 pixels. Also, Facebook has a very strict rule that only 20 percent of the image can contain text. Keep these guidelines in mind when creating your images.

If you simply can't create an image you like, Facebook does offer a convenient alternative. Instead of uploading an image, you have the option to "Find Images." This opens up a search box, where you can search for photographs to match your message (provided for free through a contract between Facebook and Shutterstock). (See figure 4.7.)

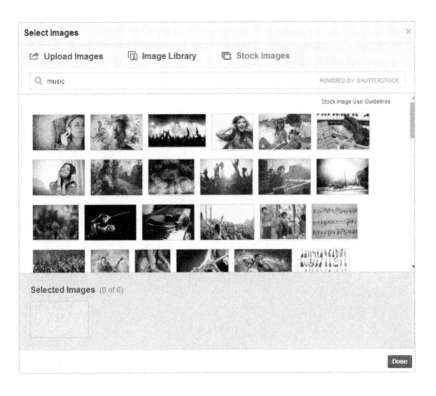

FIGURE 4.7

Shutterstock photo collection

After choosing an image, or images, you'll need to create the copy for the ad. (See figure 4.8.)

The right side of the screen is the ad itself, with the image we chose in the previous step. This ad is using an image Micah created specifically for this example. (Thanks Micah!)

The Headline shows up directly underneath the image. As its name indicates, this is the line you're trying to use to catch users' attention. You're only allowed twenty-five characters for a Headline, so choose your words carefully. In this example, our Headline is "Free Music Now!" It's direct, it tells the complete story, and it offers three things that people like: immediacy, free, and music.

The copy from the Text box shows up directly above the ad. It's basically the same as the status area above an image in a post. In our ad, we chose, "Download free music every week from your public library! It's yours to keep!" With our text, we reiterated our Headline message with

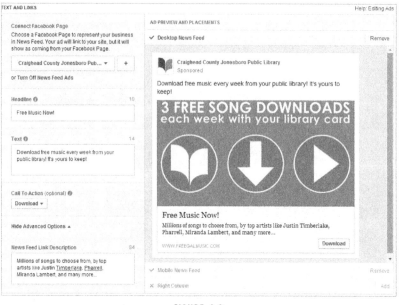

FIGURE 4.8

Creating copy

additional clarity, by letting people know that it was downloadable music and that it was ongoing, every week. We also answered the most frequently asked question about our downloadable music with the statement, "It's yours to keep!"

Underneath the text box is a "Call to Action" button. Choosing one of these will create a button on your ad, encouraging people to click it. You won't always necessarily use this feature, but in our case, we're going to choose the Download button, since we're encouraging our users to download music.

Clicking "Show Advanced Options" reveals another text box, "News Feed Link Description." Text in this box will show up directly below the Headline. It's a place to provide additional information about the library's music service. In this space, we highlight some of the artists available through Freegal: "Millions of songs to choose from, by top artists like Justin Timberlake, Pharrell, Miranda Lambert, and many more." We're pointing out the vast selection available as well as highlighting popular artists from various genres. We want to do this to appeal to as wide an audience as possible, to let people know there's something for everyone.

Underneath the ad, on the right side of the screen, you can click on "Mobile News Feed" or "Right Column" to see what the ad will look like when displayed in those areas as well.

NOTE: There may be times when you don't want an ad to show up on a particular platform. For instance, if you wanted to have patrons fill out a form online, you might not want that ad showing up on mobile devices, because people are less likely to fill out a form on their smartphone. At the same time, remember that limiting platforms also limits reach, so you're probably going to wind up paying more per click. Regardless, if you ever want to keep an ad from showing up on a particular platform, simply click "remove" and it won't show up there.

Before we move on to the next section of ad creation, I want to take a moment to emphasize the importance of quality images and copy for the success of your ads. It's no different than the posting strategy we talked about in the last chapter. You're trying to create content that will compel Facebook users to take action.

Don't rush the process and whip up an ad in just a few minutes. Think about what you want to say, how you want to say it, what images are going to reflect your message, and most of all, who you're trying to reach. This part of the process could mean the difference between paying $0.75 per click and $0.25 per click. That's a lot of clicks.

Once you're happy with your ad, you'll move on to the Audience section, where you'll determine who will see your ad. (See figure 4.9.)

There are a number of parameters available in the demographics section. For the sake of our example, we're going to be targeting everyone within a 25-mile radius of Jonesboro.

On the right side of the screen, the potential reach shows the number of available Facebook users within your target audience; in CCJPL's case, 68,000 people. As you adjust different demographic parameters, you'll notice this number change, reflecting the limitations you've defined.

When setting demographics, think about who you're trying to reach and set your parameters accordingly. If you have an event that's just for women, or just for teens, adjust those parameters accordingly. This will

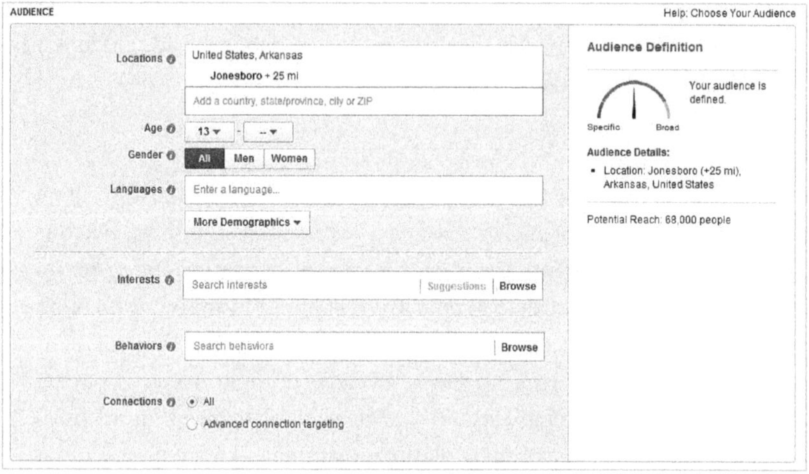

FIGURE 4.9

Set your demographics

help you avoid wasting potential clicks on people for whom the ad isn't intended.

Since we're promoting free music to everyone in our service area, the 25-mile radius around Jonesboro is pretty reflective of that audience. You could also define your audience by zip code, reduce or increase the radius around your community, add additional communities, and so on.

After setting up the demographics for your target audience, you're ready to set your ad budget and duration and launch your ad. (See figure 4.10.)

The "Campaign and Ad Set" section is where you'll decide how much you want to spend on your ad and how long your ad will run.

You can also change the name of this particular ad campaign and ad set (you can actually create multiple ads under one campaign . . . different ads scheduled to run at different times, for instance). Here, we've called our Campaign "Freegal Ad" and left the Ad Set name "Jonesboro—13+," reflecting the target audience of the ad.

By default, the Budget is set to "Per Day" and the schedule is set to run the ad continuously, starting today. Choosing this option would set the ad to run indefinitely, until you manually stopped the ad, spending the designated budget each day. We'll change the Budget to "Lifetime Budget" and set the amount to $50. We'll also set the duration of the ad. In this case, we'll run the ad for one week.

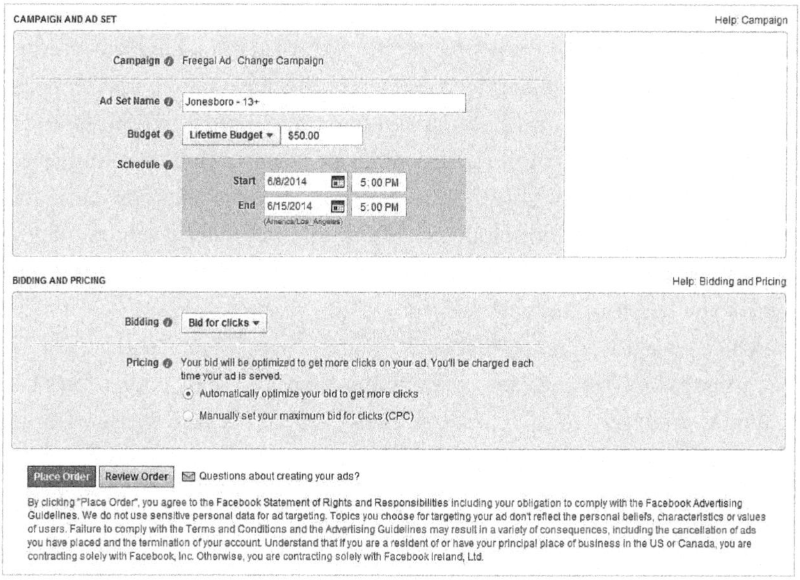

FIGURE 4.10

Set your ad budget

NOTE: Facebook will spread the exposure of your ad pretty much evenly over the duration of your ad. Since you're actually paying for the ad based on the number of times it shows to users, Facebook will use approximately $7.15 of the budget each day. Based on our previous calculations ($50 reaching 10,000 people), that means your ad will be seen by roughly 1,400 people each day.

The community interest in your event or program, as well as the quality of your ad, will determine how many people click your ad, and thereby determine your cost per click.

The next section is "Bidding and Pricing," and is where things can get complicated if we let them. The two bidding options are "Bidding for Clicks" and "Bidding for Impressions." Since we want people clicking our ad and going to our website to download music, we'll be "Bidding for Clicks."

In the "Pricing" section, we have the option of allowing Facebook to automatically optimize our bid to get the most clicks, or manually setting up our maximum bid for clicks (CPC). In simplest terms, this determines whether we want to let Facebook use its algorithm to manage our bidding or we want to manage our bids ourselves. Because you're just learning how all of this works and ad management gets pretty tedious if you're manually managing your bidding, we'll leave this option on automatic.

While you might be able to squeeze out a few more clicks by managing the bids yourself, Facebook does a good job of competitively managing your bidding for you. The savings you'd see from doing it yourself aren't worth the hassle of having to do so.

Once everything is set, just click "Place Order." The first time you set up an ad, you'll have to set up a payment method. Facebook offers two payment methods, credit card and PayPal, so you'll have to use a library credit card or set up a library PayPal account. Once you've already created your first ad, your orders will be placed automatically and your chosen payment method will be used.

Once your ad is placed, it will be reviewed by Facebook and usually receive approval within a few minutes.

Being able to create and schedule ads in this way will allow your library to plan its marketing strategy in advance and have the ads built, approved, and scheduled to run at their designated times. It's perfectly reasonable to determine your Facebook ads for an entire month and build all the ads at one time.

As I said previously, once your first ad is created, you'll have an option on the left side of your Facebook home screen, "Ads Manager" (mine is located just below "Events" under my profile picture). This is where you'll go to, well, manage ads.

Selecting your campaign brings up the management page for that campaign, and clicking on the ad brings up the management page for the specific ad (remember, you can run more than one ad in a campaign, but here we only have one ad in the campaign). This is where all those numbers come from I've been telling you about all chapter. Since we didn't actually run the ad we built in the example, we'll look at the page for the CCJPL concert ad. (See figure 4.11.)

You'll notice the number of website clicks, reach, frequency (the average number of times the ad was shown to each person), total spent, and average cost per website click prominently displayed in the middle of the screen, along with a graph detailing the ad's daily performance.

FIGURE 4.11

Ad management page

NOTE: To calculate the total number of times your ad appears (impressions), multiply the total reach (the number of unique people reached) by the frequency (the number of times each person saw the ad). In the case of the concert ad, it had a reach of 11,290 people and a frequency of 1.55. Therefore, the ad actually showed up a total of 17,500 times.

You can also edit your ad from this page. You can edit an ad at any time. So, if you see that your ad isn't performing well, you might try changing the image or coming up with a new Headline.

On the left side of the screen (not pictured in the image . . . there wasn't room) is the Ads Management menu. It contains options for creating new ads, managing your campaigns, adjusting settings, viewing reports, and so on.

The reporting tools are robust, and contain virtually every piece of data available about your ad. These reports can be easily exported to Excel and distributed to management for review.

YEAH, HOW DO I EXPLAIN THIS TO MY BOSS?

True, you aren't likely to keep your boss's attention long enough to explain all this to them.

In the website chapters, I discussed how we used stories to help leadership understand how people could use our website and mobile site, since understanding the technologies behind the sites was less important than understanding the impact the sites would have on our patrons.

In the case of a Facebook ad, instead of explaining all that stuff you just read about how it works, explain the value the ad can bring to the services you provide.

Let's go back to that Freegal ad we just built and use it to explain to our boss why a Facebook ad is a good value for the library and the community. We're going to be using a lot of what we've learned so far, so I hope I've explained this thoroughly enough and you've kept up.

Freegal's standard contract with libraries offers an annual subscription that allows each library card holder to download three songs every week, while the library pays a flat rate annually. It's the kind of service that's a natural promotional opportunity. Everyone loves free music, so you have a wide range of potential users. And since you pay a flat annual rate, it doesn't cost you more money if more people use the service. It practically begs to be promoted.

NOTE: I do have permission from Brain Downing, CEO of Library Ideas, LLC, to speak about their service, Freegal. We've discussed the numbers I'll be using in this example and he's agreed they are acceptable. I don't want anyone to think I'm giving away trade secrets or speaking out of turn.

So, you've got to convince your boss of all the stuff you've read. Here's the argument:

A $50 Facebook ad will reach about 10,000 people. Free music is a pretty great offer, but we'll be conservative and say that 2 percent of the people who saw the ad went to our website and downloaded music (2.9 percent clicked on the ad to learn more about the concerts, so the 2 percent is conservative). That's 200 people.

Each of those people gets to download three songs. So, that's 600 songs downloaded. The average cost to download a song from iTunes, Amazon, or elsewhere is basically $1.00. By running a $50 ad for a week, your library has saved your community $600. That's a substantial return on investment. But that's just one week. What happens if those same people download their three songs for an entire year? That's 31,200 songs, or $31,200 in savings, from a $50 ad.

That's how the ad shows an ROI for the community. They are able to get the music for free from the library, rather than paying for it. Now let's look at how the ad shows an ROI for the library.

I mentioned earlier that Freegal's contract requires the library to pay a flat rate annually and this was a good thing for the library. For this example, and with Brain's permission, we'll say that our contract is $10,000 a year. We'll also say we haven't done a great job of promoting the service and we're averaging about 10,000 downloads per year. (You may be doing better. This is an example. Just bear with me). So, we're basically paying the same price per song, $1.00, as our patrons would be paying if they bought the songs from iTunes. That's not being a very effective resource for our community. There's no value there.

Now let's factor in those 31,200 songs we got for our $50 ad. That would give us a total of 41,200 songs, while our contract is still $10,000. That works out to $0.24 per song, while increasing the value, the ROI, of our Freegal contract by over 300 percent. That's being a very effective resource for our community. Not bad, Facebook.

I'm well aware that I've made a lot of assumptions in this argument, and the numbers there aren't really attainable. But that's part of the beauty of the argument.

It doesn't matter if the boss tries to tell you not everyone is going to download all their songs every week, or not all 200 people who went to the website would have a library card, or not everyone who downloaded music would have otherwise bought it.

No matter their argument, it's impossible for them to strip away enough value to say it isn't worth it to run the $50 ad. Remember, we aren't trying to trick anyone into anything. We're trying to help them do the right thing. We shouldn't really have to sell the idea to them. It's just math. We've just framed it in a way that's easier to understand.

Using Facebook advertising as a public awareness tool can increase value in virtually any service we offer. Our ROI is value-based. We aren't a business. We're never going to show a profit. We measure our return on investment based on utilization. The more people who use our services, the more valuable those services become, both socially and financially.

OK, WE'RE CONVINCED

I certainly hope so.

Between these last two chapters, I've taken up a significant portion of this book to talk about Facebook. That isn't by accident. Facebook isn't a social media toy. It's an important tool that libraries need to take advantage of. It offers exceptional opportunities to reach our patrons and allows us to measure results in real and tangible ways.

In closing, I'll ask you to consider one other benefit of all this promotion. What impact would it have, from an advocacy perspective, for your community to know, on an ongoing basis, that the library is active and vibrant, with a variety of offerings for everyone? How might that awareness impact the decision of a potential voter if the library winds up on a ballot initiative? That's got to be worth $50.

SUMMARY POINTS

- Facebook advertising is the most efficient public awareness tool available to libraries today.
- Running Facebook ads to gain page likes is no longer an effective strategy.
- A $50 ad reaches approximately 10,000 people.
- Ads reach Facebook users whether they are fans of the library or not.
- Increasing utilization increases the value of a service.
- Direct promotion of library services creates "hard ROI."
- Reach is the number of unique users who saw your ad.
- Cost per website click is indicative of ad success and interest in the library service being promoted.
- Don't underestimate the impact of quality images and copy on an ad's success.
- Don't try to explain the details of Facebook advertising to decision makers. Use the Freegal story to show the value of the ad.

- Study this chapter until you have a firm understanding of it. It may be the most valuable chapter in this book.

NOTE: If it isn't obvious, I believe in the power of Facebook as a public awareness tool for libraries. However, I would be remiss if I didn't include some discussion of other social media platforms.

Libraries have built presences on virtually every social media platform. However, not all social media environments are created equally. I believe there are currently two platforms worth discussing, other than Facebook, where libraries can build valuable and sustainable relationships with their patrons. Unfortunately, we aren't using either of them. So, I've asked a couple of experts to contribute to this work and discuss Twitter and Pinterest. In appendix A, Ned Potter discusses strategies for libraries interested in developing a successful presence on Twitter. And in appendix B, Josh Tate writes about how to incorporate Pinterest into your library's public awareness efforts.

5

MARKETING IN THE "REAL WORLD"

WHILE SOCIAL MEDIA are a cost-effective marketing tool, libraries should still market in traditional mediums as well. Though there has been a huge shift to online content, people still drive cars, go to restaurants, watch television, and listen to the radio. Social media supplements marketing in physical spaces but are not intended to replace real-world marketing altogether.

The first part of this chapter will discuss some of the traditional mediums, such as newspapers, radio, and television, which remain fairly steady, even as we move to digital sources for information. In the other sections, we'll discuss techniques many libraries aren't using to their fullest potential, if at all.

We'll discuss approaches such as annual campaigns, strategies for creating effective marketing materials, and ways to distribute that material for the greatest success in reaching the community. Successful promotion of anything, whether it's hamburgers or library services, is based on the quality of the creative content, needed in order to capture the attention of the target audience, and the appropriate distribution of that content so it is seen by the target audience.

Unfortunately, many libraries choose not to budget for marketing at all. Libraries are often willing to pay upwards of 95 percent of their annual budgets for staffing and materials, yet allocate no funds whatsoever to make the community aware of the materials available for their use or the events and services the library's staff provides. McDonald's might make the best hamburger in the world, but without a successful marketing campaign, no one is going to know about that hamburger. Your library might provide the very best services of any organization in your community, but it makes no difference if you don't make the community aware of those services. A library having a $4 million budget shouldn't only allocate $5,000 to making the community aware of all the wonderful events and services that $4 million was spent to provide. Consider the number of costly books in your library that never get borrowed or the number of duplications in resources in digital and hard-copy format that are underused. Some of those moneys could be shifted to a promotional budget to help the community become more aware of the value their library has for them.

This chapter challenges libraries to allocate funding and make a concerted effort to engage their communities and promote their offerings.

NEWSPAPERS, RADIO, TV

Newspapers have lost readership in the last decade or so, with many readers moving to online sources for news, especially national news. Radio and television stations are fighting for an increasingly fragmented audience. However, newspapers, radio, and television stations are all still good partners for libraries. All three mediums are quite effective, especially in their local markets. In working with these mediums, a library's goal is to provide news stories, not purchase advertising space.

Libraries should cultivate strong, mutually beneficial relationships with each of these organizations. Libraries enjoy a unique status with these mediums because we are not-for-profit organizations that aid our communities. Newspapers, radio stations, and television stations are often also very supportive of their communities and want to be viewed as community helpers. Considering this, the library can provide free, ready-to-use content to these mediums and invite each to events for coverage of positive community news.

Whenever working with the media or writing a press release, be sure to include the who, what, why, when, where, and how of the event or service and contact information for the person in charge. Make it easy for the person receiving the information to immediately understand its importance and where it fits in with the rest of their news coverage. Make your message complete enough to publish or read on the air as it is and enticing enough to attract a reporter or photographer if possible.

Newspapers. Library events can often appear on newspaper front pages, especially smaller papers, on slow news days. They'll be buried inside if there is any other news for the front page, however. And there is no way to anticipate what will be a slow news day. Always keep your local paper informed about your events or new services. Provide them a calendar in advance, and give the lifestyles editor a call or e-mail if you know a good photo opportunity is coming. For-profit organizations must buy ads for promotion and hope to attract a reporter or editor to write an article for greater coverage. They can't write or buy an article. Libraries, on the other hand, can write their own articles and shoot their own photos to give to newspapers for publication. Newspapers often welcome well-written articles as local features or filler. Library news fills space the newspaper won't have to pay a reporter to fill. Provide good photos with articles to increase the likelihood of publication and better placement. Make the photos candid shots of patrons when possible. Newspapers often avoid photos of posed people looking at cameras and holding trophies or checks. Ask your local editor how he or she would like to receive news from the library and provide it in that format, and in advance, so your material is ready any time there is a news lull.

Radio. Radio marketing is most effectively done through on-air interviews or stories provided by library staff, rather than through the purchase of relatively expensive on-air spots. Much like with the newspaper, the library should keep radio stations informed about events or services in order to provide them with community news. Our library sends staff for live, on-the-air interviews with the morning show hosts of two local radio stations twice monthly, to discuss events and services at the library. Again, we get this opportunity because we are not-for-profit and are sharing community news on the community's radio stations. Another opportunity to promote the library is to coordinate a live remote with the radio station for one or two major library events a year. Radio stations have production costs associated with live feeds, such as hauling equipment and paying their on-air personalities. Because of the costs, the library can offer to promote the radio's participation as a sponsor of the events through other marketing channels the library uses, such as its website, Facebook page, and printed promotional materials. This benefits the station in that it projects an image of community service and goodwill on their part by donating their resources to help the library, and therefore, the community.

TV. Television ads are extremely expensive relative to most library budgets and generally not an option. But all local news stations offer community coverage that includes library events. Libraries should pitch news stories and make staff available for interviews. Our library has scheduled monthly appearances on our local television station's morning news program to discuss our events and services. This is a good way to promote events in advance. We also make staff available for interviews whenever the station wants, and invite the station to major events to capture footage and produce stories for the evening news, which is akin to making it to the newspaper's front page. While viewers normally see this footage after the event, when it's too late to participate in that particular event, it shows what's happening at the library and increases community awareness of the library in general and the many things we have to offer. Get to know your local news teams and learn what will attract them to the library and what opportunities you might provide that best suit their medium. These relationships have reciprocal value for the library and the news media, as well as community value in the exposure they provide.

OVERARCHING THEME

One key to successful marketing for any organization is to make your promotional material memorable. It must be unique so it doesn't get lost in the clutter of all the other advertising that inundates people on a daily basis. Libraries can accomplish this without having to come up with completely original material to promote every library event. We at CCJPL select an annual overarching theme for all the marketing we'll do in a given year.

An overarching theme can basically be any promotional style a library determines will stand out among other advertising in the community. Examples of effective themes include:

- Typography, in which the words are also the art
- Vintage, reminiscent of 1950s and 1960s artwork, or the old Route 66 advertisements

- Retro, reflective of the advertising style of a generation currently popular as a throwback, such as 1970s, 1980s, or 1990s styles
- Street art, which must be done tastefully but is quite powerful in catching people's attention
- Internet memes, which are popular ideas, images, or trends that circulate on the Internet quickly and become something of pop cultural phenomena

Our 2012 marketing campaign took advantage of the popularity of Internet eCards. We used this overarching theme for our print and digital marketing content throughout the year. ECards have simple compositions with sketches accompanied by brief, usually humorous, text. Part of their effectiveness in print material is achieved as a result of people's expectation of only seeing eCards in digital format. Thus they capture the audience's attention when seen outside their expected medium. Capturing the audience's attention is one of the biggest challenges faced in a world where people are constantly bombarded with advertising and information. (See figure 5.1.)

Selecting an overarching theme every year has two significant advantages over developing completely unique marketing material each time there's a service or event to promote.

FIGURE 5.1

2012 eCard poster for the religion section in our stacks

■ It simplifies the process of marketing individual events or services by providing a predetermined conceptual foundation from which to work. For example, when we promoted our concert series in 2012, we knew at the outset that our posters should look like eCards in order to adhere to the year's theme. This allowed us to focus on what artwork and phrases would best promote the concerts, as we already knew what style we were going to use. We settled on three ideas: a drawing of a woman singing paired with the text, "Concerts on the lawn, because the chairs kept falling off the roof"; a drawing of an old man playing a guitar with the text, "Concerts on the lawn, because what else have you got to do on a Tuesday night"; and a rock 'n' roller with the phrase, "Concerts on the lawn, the closest you'll ever get to being a groupie." We used this approach for all of our marketing material, thereby eliminating the burden of starting completely from scratch every time we had to create promotional material.

■ Using an overarching theme also benefits the library by keeping your message consistent and recognizable throughout the year. The theme builds branding. Use eye-catching art and messaging, and as you produce more materials from the theme, your audience is more likely to pay attention because they liked what you did before. They will come to immediately recognize other materials you produce throughout the year.

Changing the theme annually is probably necessary. Things don't necessarily retain their popularity long-term and we don't want new content to become dated because a style is no longer interesting. Changing themes also allows the library to come up with new and creative ways to increase community awareness, and continue to appear fresh and innovative.

BILLBOARDS

Many libraries consider billboards to be too expensive for consideration as a marketing tool. However, depending on the market, they can be very cost-effective, given the level of exposure they provide for the library. Billboard vendors will provide a list of all available billboard locations and statistics on traffic patterns for their billboards throughout the community. Traffic volume and location determine the cost of leasing billboards.

Price also fluctuates with the market. Vendors are likely to negotiate price if they have a number of billboards not currently in use, because a billboard with advertising on it at any price is far more preferable to vendors than a blank one. It's at least worth finding out what billboards are available in the library's community and asking what kinds of deals might be negotiated.

In 2012 our library advertised on four billboards around the outskirts of the city. We negotiated a deal with the billboard company for a six-month contract. In return for the six-month contract, the vendor agreed to keep our advertising up beyond the contract until someone else rented the space. Each of these billboards remained up for eight to ten months, as a result.

In 2013 we changed our strategy a bit, opting for higher-traffic areas, but maintaining the cost by dropping from four to three billboards while keeping the same six-month contract. But we also negotiated that if someone else leased the space at the end of our contract, we'd have our boards moved to another available location for an additional six months at no additional cost, essentially getting three billboards for one year at half price. This was mutually beneficial, as the billboard company could keep material on its boards while we received the additional marketing exposure, in addition to having the opportunity to promote the library in a new location.

Consider this example in evaluating the cost of billboards. At CCJPL, the average drive-by traffic for one of our billboard locations is 25,000 people a day. Over the course of a year, that billboard will have been seen approximately 9,125,000 times. Each of our billboards costs $3,000 for 12 months. That's $8.22 a day. At that rate, the library is spending .0003 cents per exposure opportunity.

The contrarian argument is that the vast majority of this traffic will be the same people every day. However, this is actually a good thing for the library. It's a yearlong reinforcement to people that they should visit the library. Compared to the cost of direct mailing at about 30 cents per address, for instance, billboards might be considered an excellent marketing investment. The level of exposure is worth it, whether a library can buy one billboard or a dozen.

Most billboard advertising is unfortunately nothing more than roadside visual pollution. People are anesthetized to seeing 99-cent hamburger ads and offers for $49 motel rooms. They see big numbers all along the roadside and pay no attention to them. A library billboard must be something different to be successful. The drawings and funny quips from our 2012 eCard campaign were unexpected on billboards and drew lots of attention. It was the sort of thing someone would see and mention to their coworkers once they got to work. We received a tremendous amount of positive feedback, as they were something completely unique and entertaining.

Our library's overarching theme for 2013 was art typography. We called it "WORDS," and the promotional messages were delivered as part of the art itself. Having chosen a funny marketing approach the previous year, we opted for something elegant and artistic that would catch the community's imagination in a different way. People will look at art, and billboards can be art, not just advertising. The billboards for WORDS were "Choose Your Adventure," "Tell Your Story," and "Find Your Rhythm," all in stylish typography. The phrases were evocative and intended to elicit a feeling of connectedness with the library, not as a static place, but as a facilitator of fun and activity for the community. We want the community to see the library as something to do, not just a place to be. (See figure 5.2.)

Because of the cost of each billboard, we don't promote specific library events or services. Instead, we try to instill curiosity and sell the library as an idea, as something they should check out. Billboards should have a big emotional impact. Regardless of a library's overarching theme, it's important to ensure the billboards look nothing like the others along the roadside. We've found that simple text and images, sort of maximizing minimalism, tend to cut through the clutter and can have a greater emotional impact on the viewer.

POSTERS

Library posters are extremely common. There are posters available for any number of annually celebrated library events, like Summer Reading Club, Banned Books Week, and National Library Card Signup Month. Many libraries buy preprinted posters from vendors to hang in the libraries, such as the "READ" posters that have been around for some time, or the "@YourLibrary" posters. These posters do look nice inside the building. However, they do little to brand or market the specific library, and their reach extends only to those who already come to the library, your regular patrons.

FIGURE 5.2

2013 WORDS campaign billboards

Some libraries make posters in-house to market events. Unfortunately, these posters often consist of little more than clip art and facts about the event being promoted. In many cases they are posted only in the library as well. Again, these posters will inform your current patrons, but they do nothing to draw in the larger community.

For successful community marketing, posters should be distributed outside the library and must be just as eye-catching and engaging as billboards, and for the same reasons, to attract crowds to your events. The concert posters mentioned earlier in this chapter are examples of an approach that elicits a good response. The library should have a strategy for getting them out into the community and in front of potential new patrons. There are a good number of businesses and organizations in every community that will welcome the library to hang posters in their windows if you'll only ask. Places libraries should ask to hang posters include restaurants, bars, convenience stores, malls, bowling alleys, skating rinks, community centers, recreation centers, laundromats, and the list goes on. An eye-catching poster placed in the window of a popular restaurant has the potential to reach thousands of people a week, people who aren't necessarily library patrons and who wouldn't have otherwise known about the event being promoted. Even if someone isn't interested in a particular event, a poster that catches their eye is still a great promotion for the library. It's branding, and keeps the library in the front of people's minds. If people see library posters all over town, they see that the library is active, engaged in the community, and interested in attracting more patrons. (See figure 5.3.)

FIGURE 5.3

2013 summer movie series poster

Marketing posters are an inexpensive way to boost attendance at events. The more you distribute, the greater opportunity for success of library programs. Over the course of three years, CCJPL went from having very light programming attendance to having to require registration to ensure we had room and staff available to manage the number of people wanting to participate. We accomplished this by providing quality programming, quality marketing content, and broad distribution throughout the community.

When returning to take down posters after an event, try to have another one ready to hang in its place. This eliminates having to return to seek permission for the next one later and reduces the chances that you'll be told no or that someone else's poster will replace yours in the window. Even if you don't have a new upcoming event to promote, take the opportunity to create a poster that promotes a new service that the community might not be aware of, like e-books or free music. Given the number of programs and events offered at the library, posters will make up a significant portion of the materials produced by the library. Make sure they are attractive and enticing.

POSTCARDS

Postcards are, in essence, simply miniature versions of your posters. One of the advantages of printing and distributing postcards is they can have the creative work on the front and all the event information on the back. This allows for the artwork and marketing to be showcased while still delivering all of the pertinent facts about the program or event.

Postcards should be placed at every customer service point in the library. They should also be placed in every bag or given to every patron at checkout. Staff needs to be aware of what event is currently being promoted and actively engage patrons about attending, using the postcard as a take-home reminder for the patron. Current library events or programs are also a great time to inform patrons about upcoming events. For instance, if the library is hosting a concert this month and has an author visiting next month, go ahead and have the postcards made up for the author visit and hand them out during the concert.

Staff should distribute postcards in the community as well. Most businesses aren't as likely to be as ok with having a stack of postcards next to their cash register as they would be about hanging a poster in the window. However, most libraries have some sort of outreach program or other community engagement outside the building. These are opportunities to hand out postcards and promote upcoming events. Does your library do storytimes at day care centers? If so, staff should take advantage of the opportunity to hand out postcards to all the children as well as leave some for the day care center to give to parents. Does your library participate in any civic clubs such as Rotary or Kiwanis? This is an opportunity to hand out postcards that club members can take back to their respective businesses and give to other employees. Other opportunities include business expos, back-to-school events, or other places the library is likely to set up a booth. In these situations, don't just sit at the booth and allow passersby to pick up postcards. Take advantage of the chance to visit other booths and market the library to the vendors as well. At worst, most communities have areas that are busy during lunchtime and the library can schedule staff to go out a couple of times a week prior to an event and hand out postcards to people on the street during their lunch hour.

As with other marketing materials, appealing artwork and a good tagline will motivate people to read the card and thus be more likely to remember what the library is promoting. Like posters hung in store windows around town, thorough postcard distribution outside the library is sure to increase program attendance and expose new patrons to the library.

I've been questioned about sending postcards as direct mail. I disagree with this approach for a couple of reasons. First, it's relatively costly to do direct mailings to a significant number of people throughout the community. Second, the problem with bulk mailing is that it likely winds up being delivered on the same day as most of the "junk" mail and is likely to wind up getting tossed into the trash with it as well. The distribution methods mentioned above are more effective in getting the information in front of as many eyes as possible. Parents are more likely to look at something sent home from a day care center. Civic group members are more likely to read something given to them at a meeting. And people attending business expos or back-to-school events are there to learn more about what is available in the community. These sorts of interactions also allow for a human element in the hand-to-hand exchange and an opportunity to answer questions or provide additional information about the library.

BOOKMARKS

Bookmarks are the oldest and most common promotional items that libraries give to patrons. This is understandable, given that libraries lend books, and readers likely need something to mark their page while reading. However, bookmarks come with the same challenges as in-house posters and postcards. They're only reaching people already coming into the library.

That's not to say libraries should stop providing bookmarks, because patrons still need to mark their places in books, and they appreciate it if the library is providing attractive bookmarks. However, we also need to be taking advantage of the marketing space available.

Libraries often order preprinted bookmarks in bulk from any number of sources. These bookmarks may promote reading in general, but they do little to promote the individual library and fail to provide any specific information the library wants to share with patrons. These preprinted bookmarks cause libraries to miss a valuable marketing opportunity. A bookmark without any of the library's information may as well be a sticky note, a receipt, a napkin, or anything else a patron would use to mark their place.

At CCJPL, we design many of our bookmarks to reflect the year's overarching marketing theme. In 2013 we simply took our billboard designs, modified the layout a bit, and used that artwork for our bookmarks. As with postcards, we put library information on the back. Since we don't necessarily use bookmarks to promote specific events, but rather the library as a whole, we include general library information on the back, such as the address, phone number, hours of operation, website address, and Facebook page. Our goal is to provide patrons with information that will expose them to the wide range of offerings the library provides, and the bookmark serves as a pretty handy reminder to patrons that we're a lot more than just the book they're currently reading.

While custom bookmarks can be slightly more expensive than bulk-ordered, unbranded bookmarks, the opportunity to provide patrons with information specific to the individual library far outweighs any cost difference between the two. As with postcards, bookmarks should be made available and handed out whenever possible in the community.

DRINK COASTERS

One of the most unique means by which we've started promoting the library has been the creation of a set of drink coasters. As is often the case, inspiration came from necessity. Several of us were at Skinny J's, a local restaurant in town, on a Wednesday night, trivia night. I picked up my beer to take a drink, and the water on the outside of the glass dripped down my arm. My initial reaction was one of frustration, thinking these people really need some drink coasters.

Then I realized what a great promotional tool coasters could be if the restaurant would let us provide them. I spoke with the manager and she said she'd love for the library to provide the restaurant with drink coasters. (See figure 5.4.)

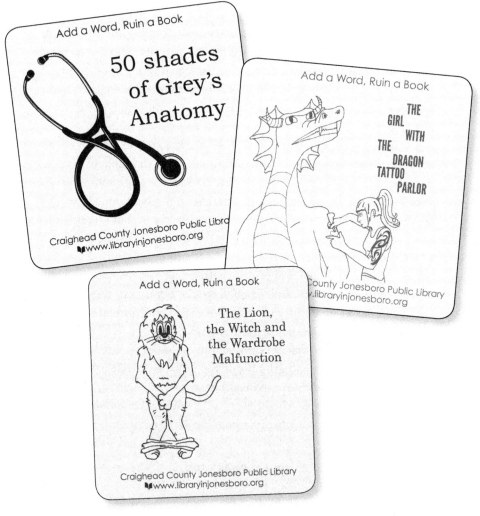

FIGURE 5.4

Coasters

The logic behind the promotion was pretty simple. With a good "hook" that would get people's attention, and our website at the bottom of the coaster, we would basically have a captive audience from the time a customer placed their drink order until the time they got their food. Most people often spend this time looking at their smartphones. This seemed to create an ideal promotional ecosystem. Given that we had a very well-designed mobile website, the idea was that the funny coasters would entice the diners to check it out, and we could go from promotion to delivery in real-time.

GIVEAWAY ITEMS

Libraries frequently give a variety of inexpensive items to people in the community, at business expos, community festivals, back-to-school programs, basically anywhere the library has an opportunity to set up a booth. Unfortunately, we are frequently challenged in our decisions on what items to buy because we are forced to keep the cost per item low. This can result in our giving away things recipients are not likely to use. Think carefully before ordering the cheapest thing you can find. Often, for a few pennies more or with just a little thought, you can extend the life and increase the impact of your gift.

Take pens for instance. Sure, patrons will take the cheap pen with the library logo, but they're likely to just bury it in a utility drawer when they get home. On the other hand, if the library invested a little more money in quality pens, people are far more likely to use the pen, because people tend to treasure good pens. A small increase in spending can have a huge impact on the success of a giveaway item. Instead of a pen that gets relegated to a drawer already full of pens, you now have individuals actually using the pen the library provided, giving them a constant, in-hand reminder of where they got it. People appreciate the company that was willing to spend a little more to give them a good pen to use. Those pens stay in the cup on top of the desk when not in use, not in the back of a junk drawer.

Notepads are another example of where a small increase in spending can have a significant impact on the marketing success of the giveaway. Rather than regular notepads, libraries might give away sticky notepads, making sure to include the library's name, logo, and website on them. For better or worse, many of us are guilty of having too many reminder sticky notes posted in our homes or offices. If the library gives away a notepad people will use and includes the library's website address across the top or bottom, that helps serve as a reminder to check out the library, thus exposing them to library services. Another notepad idea is notepads with magnets on the back. These can be hung on refrigerators and be used for grocery lists, for instance, and remind people about the library every time they make a note.

Buttons are also popular and are another opportunity to market the library. Like posters and bookmarks, though, avoid bulk-order buttons with generic text, such as "I love my library," in favor of customized buttons with a cool image, catchy phrase, and your website along the bottom. Patrons are more likely to appreciate, wear, and display cool custom buttons.

Our patrons often need ear buds for use on our public computers, and the quantity we need to provide for patrons makes customization cost prohibitive. For in-house use, we buy the least expensive ear buds available. However, as marketing tools, we order ear buds that come in small nylon bags attached to a key-ring holder. This gives us an opportunity to market on the bag with our logo and web address, and even if the patron doesn't continue to use the relatively inexpensive ear buds that come with it, they still might store their new ear buds in our branded bag, which can help keep the library at the front of their consciousness every time they use their ear buds.

There are many, many other examples of good giveaway items. The thing to keep in mind is whether or not you're giving away something with a chance people will use it, or you're giving away something that people are willing to take because it's free, but are likely to wind up throwing in the trash or some drawer when they get home. The idea isn't to give things away just for the sake of gift giving. There is no return on the library's investment on items that are thrown in the trash or stashed in drawers, never to be seen again.

Use a strategic approach to selecting giveaways. Determine their cost-effectiveness by the work they'll do for you, not just their purchase price.

Spending slightly more on a far superior product and ordering items people are likely to value and use mean we are likely to achieve the desired result of continued library exposure. This is far more effective than spending less money for inferior products that are immediately cast aside and for which the return on the library's investment is essentially zero. We want our marketing giveaways to be things that will provide a constant reminder to check out the library. In order to accomplish this, we have to give away things that people actually want.

YARD SIGNS

Yard signs are effective for broad promotion of the library and can cause a lot of talk around town. They are a relatively expensive marketing tool on a per-item basis, so distribution should be handled carefully to avoid waste. Yard signs should be distributed in ways that will likely result in the most possible exposure, such as to staff, friends of the library, and patrons that are strong supporters of the library.

Yard signs should be viewed as mini-billboards, adhering to the concept of promoting the library in a general way, as an idea, rather than promoting specific services or events. Our first experience at CCJPL with library yard signs came during the 2012 presidential election. Seeing all of the candidate yard signs cluttering the corners of busy intersections, I decided it would be funny to come up with a library sign with a catchy phrase to place among them. It seemed that if we could find a way to poke fun at something the public generally didn't like, political signs, we'd get the attention of people stopped at those intersections and give them a chuckle. In a guerrilla marketing-like move, we had signs printed up with "Public Library: We don't need to run for office" and placed them among the political signs. Our signs were a huge hit and a number of patrons wanted them for their yards. (See figure 5.5.)

FIGURE 5.5
CCJPL 2012 yard sign

The signs we ordered were the corrugated plastic kind, which I'd recommend. These will last a lot longer and look a lot better than the less expensive cardboard signs. While individually expensive, printing 25–50 yard signs that are likely to remain in people's yards for several months can be an effective tool for promoting the library. Much like billboards, yard signs will be seen on a regular basis by the people driving by them and will provide a consistent reminder to check out the library.

CONCLUSION

Most of the traditional mediums discussed in this chapter aren't new to libraries. We've been using them to promote events and services for years. In many ways, the strategies and techniques covered aren't so much revolutionary as they are evolutionary. However, an evolution in practices can lead to a revolution in results.

As we've mentioned previously, CCJPL hosts four concerts at the library every summer. We've always promoted them through traditional means, but without much strategy. In 2011, we averaged 300 attendees per concert. In 2012 we created posters that we put up around town to help promote the events. Our average that year was 300 attendees. In 2013 we again hung posters around town, but we also passed out over a thousand postcards, posted several times about the concerts on Facebook, and made sure to mention it on radio and TV multiple times leading up to the events. Our average attendance per concert that year was just over 500. That's a 400 percent increase in the number of people coming to a library event in the course of two years. The only difference was our approach to increasing community awareness. We didn't just disseminate information about an upcoming event. We created engaging marketing material that presented the library as fun and the concerts as something people wouldn't want to miss.

These sorts of results are attainable by any library willing to reach out in an effective way and make the community aware of the library's programs and services. It isn't as much about doing something radically different than the things we've done in the past. It's more about being better at doing the things we're already doing. The goal is to keep the community continuously aware of the library and to do so in a way that will entice them to engage, attend, and participate.

SUMMARY POINTS

- The library should partner with newspapers, radio, and TV to provide news stories to them.
- Libraries enjoy a unique status with these mediums because we are not-for-profit organizations that aid our communities. These outlets also want to be viewed as community helpers.
- For the best placement or air times, tailor your press releases to the recipient. Make them complete, easy to use, and inviting for reporters to cover.
- Ask your local editors and newscasters how they would like to receive news from the library and provide it in that format in advance, so your material is ready any time there is a news lull.
- Radio marketing is most effectively done through on-air interviews or stories provided by library staff. Make staff available.
- All news stations offer community coverage that includes library events. Pitch news stories and make staff available for interviews.
- Select an annual overarching theme for all the marketing in a given year to simplify the process of promoting individual programs.
- Billboards can be surprisingly cost-effective, depending on the local market, and prices and terms can be negotiated.
- A library billboard must be something unique to compete with roadside visual clutter and have an emotional impact.
- Use billboards to instill curiosity and sell the library as an idea.
- Instead of ordering mass-produced posters, bookmarks, and postcards, create your own to promote *your* library.
- Distribute posters throughout the community and hang in the library.
- Give bookmarks and postcards to patrons at checkout as take-home reminders about services and upcoming programs.
- Ask staff to distribute bookmarks and postcards at community events to reach new patrons or those who haven't visited the library recently.
- Provide promotional material for children's programming to day care mangers to send home to parents.
- Appealing artwork and a good headline are essential to get patrons to read the materials.

- While custom bookmarks can be slightly more expensive than bulk-ordered, unbranded bookmarks, the opportunity to provide patrons with information specific to the individual library far outweighs any cost difference.
- Drink coasters are a great way to promote the library to a captive audience.
- Think carefully before ordering the cheapest giveaway items you can find. Often, for a few pennies more, you can extend the life and increase the impact of your gift.
- Determine the value of giveaways by the work they'll do for you, not just their purchase price.
- Yard signs are effective for broad promotion of the library and can cause a lot of talk around town.
- View yard signs as mini-billboards, adhering to your overarching theme to promote the library in a general way.
- Corrugated plastic signs last longer and look better than less expensive cardboard signs, and will pay for themselves if strategically placed.

6

MAKING PRETTY PICTURES

HAVING COVERED A number of strategies that require the creation of marketing material, many are probably wondering how a library is supposed to make all of these posters, postcards, bookmarks, and billboards. Coming up with ideas for a marketing campaign can be a challenge. But with a group of people working and brainstorming together, it can hopefully prove to be a fun, team-building process. The graphic designs for all of these ideas are another story. Most libraries aren't fortunate enough to have a graphic designer on staff.

Before taking on the task of creating marketing pieces in-house, libraries may be able to find some cost-saving alternatives. A good first option is to see if there are any freelance graphic designers in the area who would be interested in working with the library. Ask local marketing firms if they're aware of any designers looking for work and see if any of them might be interested in partnering with the library. Some designers may be willing to take on these kinds of jobs to help build their portfolio or increase exposure for their work. Also, if there's a local college in your area, check with their arts or marketing departments and find out if the library can participate in an internship program, using students to create the library's material. This is mutually beneficial, as the library gets content created for free and the student earns real-world experience, college credit, and an opportunity to start building a portfolio. You might even consider checking with the arts departments at local area high schools. You'll often find high school students who will be willing to work part-time or create individual pieces very inexpensively. In any of these instances, it's important to make sure the person creating the marketing material has a clear understanding of the library's expectations and creates work consistent with those expectations.

If none of these options are available to your library, the responsibility of creating marketing material becomes that of librarians or other staff, most of whom likely have no experience in graphic design. This doesn't mean, however, that you have to continue to settle for clip art and comic sans font on white copy paper. While this chapter isn't going to turn anyone into a graphic designer, it is intended to provide some basic understanding of design principles, with which any library can create attractive, engaging marketing pieces.

BRANDING

To borrow a common phrase from the marketing world, branding is more than just a logo. Branding is about creating an emotional connection between the library and its community. It's part of the culture of the organization, in the way you conduct yourself as a service institution, the image you create for yourself through your marketing and public awareness efforts, and the impact you have on the people whose lives you touch. Everything you do is part of building a brand identity for the library. When creating intuitive websites, adding new digital or physical services, humanizing the library on social media, or developing an engaging annual marketing campaign, you're telling a story of what the library is and the value it has in people's lives.

While branding is about much more than just a logo, the logo plays a very important role in the branding process. The library's logo is the symbol of the library's brand. It's the visual representation of that emotional connection. (See figure 6.1.)

FIGURE 6.1
CCJPL logo

That's why every single piece of marketing material that leaves the library should have the library's logo on it. If everything that goes out of the library always includes the logo, over time, the community will become accustomed to seeing the logo and associating it with the feelings they have about the organization. These feelings are what encourage people to take advantage of your services, participate in your events, and tell their friends about their experiences with the library. Think about the sorts of emotions people associate with the logos of companies such as Apple or Harley Davidson, or the passion many feel at the site of their favorite sports team's logo. The library can build the same sort of emotional attachment and brand enthusiasm within its community.

In every design project, consider these emotional connections and how the marketing material ties into the brand image the library is creating. Know that the logo on each piece of marketing material is saying, "This is part of who we are."

CONSISTENCY

Each marketing piece should be an aesthetically appealing combination of fonts, artwork, colors, and information. Since our goal is to catch people's eye and then have them read the message on the marketing material, all of these components should accentuate one another.

Using stick figure drawings and an elaborate Old English font to promote something like a children's coloring contest is probably going to yield an inconsistent, unappealing promotional piece. (See figure 6.2.)

On the other hand, using a handwritten font in conjunction with the same stick figure drawings could be effective. In the image below, the text looks as though it was colored by a child, providing a harmony between the artwork and the font. (See figure 6.3.)

Not only should the elements of an individual piece be thematically consistent within the piece itself, but all of the promotional pieces created throughout the year should be consistent with the year's overarching theme as well. This consistency will help build brand recognition and hopefully make the library's marketing material immediately recognizable as the campaign moves forward.

FIGURE 6.2

Bad font choices make promotional material
less effective

FIGURE 6.3

Consistency between fonts and artwork create emotion

PLANNING

Every graphic design project starts with an idea that needs to result in a compelling and memorable finished product that successfully reaches the target audience. Planning is essential in creating a quality finished product and achieving the desired results.

The first part of planning is to make sure the design will adhere to the library's predetermined overarching theme for the year. The style of the artwork and the layout of the piece must adhere to the convention already set forth in order to maintain overall marketing consistency.

When working on a piece of marketing material, it is usually best to determine what phrase will be used as the main text portion, the headline, before determining the artwork. The headline is that clever turn of phrase you're hoping will get the viewer's attention. The headline should predicate the artwork. If the headline being used in the promotional material is, "It still counts as reading if you turn on the subtitles," which is one we used at CCJPL for one of our summer movie series posters, it wouldn't make sense to use an image of a football. (See figure 6.4.)

The medium is also an important consideration in the planning stage of a new design project. Designing a poster or postcard can allow you to use smaller fonts and provide more text than a design being created for a

FIGURE 6.4
2012 Summer Movie Series poster

billboard. Very few words should be used on a billboard, and the words will have to be bigger in relation to the overall design so the whole message can be read by people driving down the road.

Regardless of the project, the person creating the actual design itself should have a general idea of what the final piece will look like before ever beginning. Beginning the work with an idea of what imagery they want to use, color palette they are interested in, appropriate fonts for the project, and an awareness of how the marketing piece fits into the library's brand will save the designer a significant amount of development time.

FONTS

Choosing appropriate fonts for a design project can pose a challenge for people new to graphic design and experienced designers alike. Beginners should keep their font choices simple and consistent. Often we fall victim to the habit of trying to find fonts to reflect a particular theme, such as a font that might look "scary" for a poster promoting a Halloween event. Unfortunately, these types of fonts often get in the way of the message rather than clearly presenting it.

In most pieces, there should be two fonts used, one for the informational section of the piece, known as the body typeface, and one for the headline of the piece, known as the display typeface. The body typeface should almost always be a clear, easy-to-read, unobtrusive font, such as Helvetica, Arial, or Century Gothic. This font should be used for things such as the dates and times of an event, the library's website address and contact information, or other pertinent facts related to the event or service being promoted. (See figure 6.5.)

Using the same font for the headline as you used for the body text will help to ensure consistency within the work. Attention can be drawn to the headline by changing its font size and weight. Font weight is the thickness of the font relative to its height. By using the same font and simply changing its size and weight, you're letting the artwork of the piece, in combination with clear text, carry the promotional message. This is often a better delivery method than trying to choose a font style that reflects the particular theme of the material.

There are exceptions when choosing headline fonts, such as when using art typography as an overarching theme, in which case the text itself

FIGURE 6.5
Dr. Who 50th anniversary event poster

is often the art as well, or when using a theme like Pop Art, where the style of the font has been predetermined by the theme itself.

Even choosing a unique display typeface for the Halloween poster described earlier is okay, as long as the font is easy to read and isn't used for all the text in the piece. These specialty typefaces should be used sparingly in order to draw attention to a specific word or phrase. If you find yourself needing a specific-style font that isn't available with your design software, there are online resources available to download virtually any style font imaginable. www.dafont.com is an excellent resource for finding unique fonts and many of them are free for download.

NOTE: As you become more adept at creating marketing material, explore different font options and combinations. But keep in mind that when using specialty fonts, less is more. The goal is to grab the audience's attention and then deliver information. Be careful not to let the font get in the way of the information.

GRAPHICS, COLORS, AND LAYOUT

In the introduction to this chapter, I mentioned a number of options for libraries to find people within their community to provide graphic work for library marketing projects. These options will be available for many libraries, but obviously not all. If your library is unable to find anyone to create the artwork for your promotional material and doesn't have anyone on staff with artistic skills, there are other options for finding quality images for your marketing projects. A number of places online sell artwork and photographs for marketing purposes, and this artwork can be purchased at a minimal cost to the library. Istockphoto.com and shutterstock.com are great online resources with millions of images from which to choose. If your library chooses an overarching theme that is popular at all, chances are you will be able to find enough artwork based on that theme to provide you with images for an entire year's campaign.

Once artwork and fonts have been chosen for a marketing piece, it's time to choose colors for the background and text. For many people, choosing colors comes easy. I happen not to be one of those people. For those of you who are also color-challenged, there are web resources that provide color combinations to choose from. One of my favorites is color.adobe.com, where you can choose a single color and the site will build a color palette that includes additional colors that coordinate with the one you chose. By choosing one of the colors from your artwork, you can easily find background and text colors that will work well in combination.

There have been innumerable studies done on the emotional and psychological impact of color on people. According to research published by Satyendra Singh of the University of Winnipeg, "People make up their minds within 90 seconds of their initial interactions with either people or products. About 62–90 percent of the assessment is based on color alone."[1] This importance of color in decision making forces us to consider the common reactions people have to different colors.

This isn't universal, as any individual's reaction to different colors will be significantly influenced by their personal experience. However, as a general rule, these are the common emotions associated with different colors:

- Red: Action, Adventure, Fire, Lust, Power, Excitement, or Energy
- Blue: Trust, Security, Intelligence, Cleanliness, or Peace
- Yellow: Happiness, Warmth, Creativity, or Cheerfulness
- Orange: Energy, Cheerfulness, Warmth, Excitement, or Vitality
- Green: Money, Nature, Freshness, Freedom, or Tranquility
- Purple: Nobility, Wealth, Magic, Mystery, or Sophistication
- White: Innocence, Peace, Cleanliness, Purity, or Calmness
- Black: Power, Dominance, Boldness, Seriousness, Authority, or Elegance

Take advantage of the way colors impact people when working on a design project. Think about the audience, the service or event being promoted, and the way the particular piece fits into the library's overall marketing campaign. Maybe a bright, happy yellow would work well on a poster to promote a fun kid event. Perhaps reds and blacks set the best tone for a poster about an upcoming teen party. A postcard in greens or blues might be most effective to promote a knitting class geared toward older patrons.

Once a headline for the piece has been chosen, the artwork created or procured, and fonts and colors have been selected, it's time to put it all together. We've all seen library marketing material that is nothing more than a bunch of facts and pieces of clip art, randomly placed in a layout that can be printed on an 8½″ × 11″ piece of paper. People who lack experience in designing promotional material often fall prey to the idea that more is better. They'll look at something they're working on and feel like it's empty, needing just a couple more pieces of clip art or larger fonts to help fill up the page. The problem with jamming a lot of information, or color, or graphics into a design is that it often looks thrown together, a cacophony of hard-to-read information with no harmony or structure. There's nothing to catch the viewer's eye and no structure to tell them where to look. Too much information or information that lacks any flow will be jarring and visually unsettling.

White space is your friend. White space (empty space, not necessarily white) allows the various components of a piece to breathe. Viewers are only going to look at your poster, billboard, or flier for a few seconds. The different elements of a marketing piece need to be laid out in a way that is inviting to the eye, with a headline or artwork that captures the viewer's attention and a layout that allows their eyes to flow naturally through the rest of the piece. When needing to deliver information quickly, less is always more. (See figure 6.6.)

A good way to learn about laying out marketing material in an appealing way is to search the Internet for other material that is reflective of the

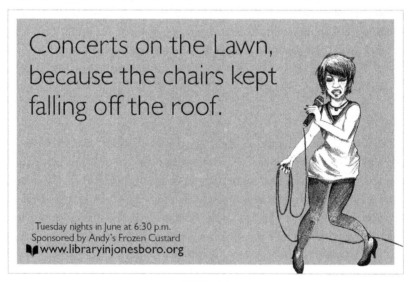

FIGURE 6.6

Our eCard posters made great use of white space

library's overarching annual theme. In the case of our eCards from our 2012 campaign, it's pretty easy to do a quick image search in the Internet for eCards and see how those are laid out and simply structure the library's promotional materials in a similar fashion.

SOFTWARE AND TRAINING

Every graphic designer will have their preferred graphic design tools they like to use in creating their designs. A great many designers work with Adobe products such as Photoshop, Illustrator, or InDesign. These and other professional design products offer a robust array of tools to complete virtually any design project. However, they are somewhat complicated for novices and can be cost-prohibitive.

Fortunately for libraries, there are a few alternatives to save significant money in purchasing these products. Software vendors will often honor academic pricing on these products for libraries, sometimes cutting the cost by as much as 80–90 percent off the retail price. Simply ask your software provider whether they offer academic pricing. Another alternative for libraries is TechSoup. TechSoup.org is a resource for nonprofit organizations and libraries through which we can obtain a wide range of software products at little to no cost. The licenses to these software products are often donated by the software development companies as part of their own goodwill and promotional efforts, making these products accessible where they would not otherwise be and exposing potential new users to their products. I strongly suggest that every library apply for a TechSoup account and take advantage of these offers to save significantly on a wide range of software solutions, not just graphics software. For libraries that do not qualify for academic pricing, cannot get a TechSoup account for whatever reason, and have no money available for software purchases, I would suggest downloading Gimp from Gimp.org. Gimp is open-source design software that is free to download and contains many of the same features as high-end professional graphics software. Further, many libraries have been successful using Microsoft Publisher. Though it lacks much of the graphic design functionality of the other software tools, its templates can be used to help with layout and structure for posters, fliers, and brochures, particularly bifold or tri-fold pieces.

Regardless of what software solution the library chooses for graphic design work, there is a learning curve that must be overcome. It's impossible to teach people how to use the wide range of tools available within the context of this book. Learning new software as well as learning good design techniques takes time and commitment. Like most anything, we become better at using the tools and create better products as we gain experience. Short of enrolling in graphic design classes or paying for classes online to learn how to use particular products, the easiest and most inexpensive way to become familiar with these software tools is to take advantage of the thousands of tutorials available on the Internet. If you have access to a service like Lynda.com, there are thousands of hours of instructional videos available, for graphic design strategies as well as specific software tools. If you don't have access to a service like Lynda.com, YouTube tutorials will teach you just about anything you'd want to know about how to use graphic design software. I learned everything I know about video editing and graphic design from watching YouTube videos and following the step-by-step tutorials. Anyone qualified to work in any significant capacity in a library should be able to use tutorial videos to train themselves enough to create quality marketing material, if they are willing to put forth the time and effort necessary to learn.

CONCLUSION

The purpose of graphic design, specifically our job of creating marketing material for the library, is to effectively engage a target audience and communicate a message. It isn't to dazzle people with our artistic talents. At the same time, creating marketing material isn't just a task to mark off of a to-do list. It can't be an afterthought. With all of the effort libraries put into programming and services, it's an injustice to ourselves and our patrons for us to create ineffective marketing material, or worse yet, no marketing material at all. The greatest program in the world will likely be poorly attended if we don't find a way to capture our audience's attention and let them know about it.

Designing captivating promotional material isn't easy. We get better at it the more we do it, the more we use the software, the more we research techniques, and the more we learn. But the benefits to our libraries and our patrons can't be understated. Our communities want to know how great we are. We just have to tell them.

SUMMARY POINTS

- If hiring a graphic designer isn't viable, look for local designers, college interns, or high school students as alternatives.
- Branding is about creating an emotional connection between the library and its community.
- Every piece of marketing material that leaves the library should have the library's logo on it.
- Each marketing piece should be an aesthetically appealing combination of fonts, artwork, colors, and information.
- All of the promotional pieces created throughout the year should be consistent with the library's overarching theme for the year.
- Choose artwork to match your message, not a message to match your artwork.
- Have a general idea of what the piece should look like before starting, including words, imagery, fonts, colors, and how the marketing piece fits into the library's branding.
- Keep font choices simple and consistent. Elaborate fonts can get in the way of the message.
- No more than two fonts should be used in most pieces, one for the headline and one for detailed information.
- There are many outside sources of quality images for your marketing projects, so avoid clip art.
- Use online resources to help select coordinating colors.
- Be aware that color evokes certain responses from audiences and use that to your design advantage.
- Keep designs simple. More is not better.
- White space is your friend.
- Software vendors and others offer money-saving opportunities to purchase professional software.
- Instructional videos are available online for learning how to use design software.

NOTE

1. Satyendra Singh, "Impact of Color on Marketing," *Management Decision* 44, no. 6: 783–89. Online at www.emeraldinsight.com/journals.htm?articleid=1558119.

7

CONVINCING THE DECISION MAKERS

MOST PEOPLE READING this book will have to get approval from someone before they can implement the ideas presented. It doesn't matter how good an idea is if you're not able to convince the decision makers within your organization to allow you to pursue it. Decision makers need to be able to understand the nature of the idea you're proposing, the value it can have for patrons, and the cost-benefit to the library.

For many libraries, the approval process will be the most challenging part of implementing the strategies mentioned in this book. Decision makers may be intimidated by technology, unfamiliar with social media, or consider marketing a waste of library resources.

The details presented in this book are specific to the Craighead County Jonesboro Public Library. However, the concepts themselves are universal. If you build a more user-friendly website, your patrons are more likely to use it. If you develop a successful social media presence, you can reach out to an ever-growing segment of your community every day. If you create compelling promotional material to market your library, you'll increase community awareness of the library, and thereby increase usage of library services.

The previous chapters are not only instructional tools on how to execute the various strategies, but also informational tools to assist you in explaining the strategies to decision makers. In this chapter, we'll cover some approaches to help navigate the approval process and create advocates out of skeptics.

WE PROFILE

Second only to knowing what you're talking about, knowing your audience is the most important part of getting approval from your decision makers.

During my hiring process at CCJPL, I had to take a personality profile test. Phyllis and David explained that it didn't impact their hiring decision. They used the personality profile for communication purposes. It was called the DiSC Personality Profile System and was administered by Jim Corter, with Corter Consulting.

Based on the answers given, a person is "scored" in four categories:

- Dominance: Places priority on the bottom line, results, strength, and confidence
- Influence: Places priority on convincing others, building individual relationships, and big ideas
- Steadiness: Places priority on team and consensus building, stability, and cooperation
- Conscientiousness: Places priority on accuracy, detail, and quality

The area in which the person "scores" the highest is considered their dominant personality type. I turned out to be an "I." I've always had an outgoing personality, so this was of little surprise. What was surprising to me, early on, was the way library staff referred to each other in casual conversation.

On any given day, you're likely to hear someone on staff referring to another staff member by their letter; "he's an 'I,'" "she's an 'S,'" "you know there's going to be a fight if we have more than one 'D' on this committee." It's become part of the culture of our organization and plays a significant role in how we interact with each other.

For instance, I know if I have a project that involves our Children's Department, I'll need to work with Kay Taylor, our youth services manager. Kay has a predominantly "S" personality, so I'll want to make sure to provide her with plenty of information and adequate time for her to process it. She's likely going to want to think it through thoroughly and consult with her staff to get their input. For Kay to support an idea, she needs time to become comfortable with it and know that her team is comfortable with it.

Our director, David, on the other hand, is an "I." When we get together to discuss something, I know that David is going to think about the big picture. Particularly in the early stages of discussion, he's going to be more focused on the overall impact an idea can have, and less concerned with the details. If we're not careful, he and I can start out talking about something as mundane as the location of a public printer, and within an hour, we're liable to be discussing how we should redesign half the library.

I don't want to imply that we only see each other as letters at the library. We're all human, with a wide range of emotions, moods, motivations, and ideas. But having a general awareness of people's personalities does help guide you when you're looking to effectively communicate.

LET'S GET TO KNOW EACH OTHER

More than likely, your library doesn't do personality profiling. It's not all that common in the industry. However, you probably do know your co-workers, supervisors, and library administration pretty well. Libraries are generally pretty close-knit. You know some of the things they like and don't like, what their expectations are, when they're in a good mood, and when it's better to discuss something tomorrow. To one degree or another, you know them personally.

If you think about the people you've worked with for any significant time, you probably have a pretty good idea of their dominant personality types. Considering their personality will help you cater your approach when attempting to get their buy-in.

But what about those decision makers you don't know? How do you approach a library board or city officials you've never met?

A lot can be learned from the questions they ask. Are they inquiring about costs, budgets, and resources? Or are they wanting to know more about the impact your idea will have on the community? Their questions are often telling you about their motivations. And their motivations are telling you about their personality. Communicating in a way that is comfortable for decision makers will help win them over at a personal level. You have an opportunity to give them *their* reasons to say yes, not just *your* reasons.

I've found that the two most effective ways to share ideas with decision makers are to either tell a story about what the idea can do for the community, or to show the financial value of implementing the idea for the library. It's a matter of knowing which approach to take with which decision makers, and for which projects.

TELL A STORY

Telling a story is extremely effective when talking about technology with laypeople. Helping people understand complicated technologies is challenging. It's easier to get approval from decision makers if you focus on what the project does, rather than how you'll approach it.

Decision makers are usually more interested in the impact of technology projects, not their detailed functions and features. They don't necessarily care about the steps you took to design the website so it would adhere to the three-click rule. But they are thrilled that even elderly patrons can easily download books and music at home without confusion. We know this is largely because of the three-click rule, but decision makers are interested in the outcome, not the mechanics.

Board members might be inspired by the idea of day care providers using the library's website to play Happy Talk stories for children at nap times. It paints a picture in decision makers' heads of children lying down on mats, drifting off to sleep, listening to stories provided by the library. That's something they'll want to be part of. It's something they can support, and their support gives them a sense of ownership. It's a story they can share with their friends. They're not interested in the conversion of cassette tapes to MP3s or the code behind the embedded media player on the site. There's nothing sweet or inspirational about all that.

The library-in-your-pocket story we used with our board when seeking approval for our mobile website is another good example of using a story to move decision makers to "yes." It's easy for them to visualize a woman downloading an e-book from the library while she's standing in the middle of a bookstore. They can appreciate how the library saved her money she would have otherwise spent.

Telling a story allows decision makers to picture an idea in action. It cuts through all of the complexities of how something works and gets to the essence of why it will be beneficial to our patrons. It's a lot easier to convince decision makers to spend thousands of dollars on a project that expands the library's reach into the homes and lives of our patrons, than it is to convince them to spend thousands of dollars on a new website.

Since it's likely that decision makers won't understand the technical nature of a project, make sure to frame your request for support in a way that appeals to them emotionally. Let them feel like they are contributing to the betterment of the library and the community. Don't make them feel like they're spending money on complicated technologies they don't understand.

SHOW VALUE

Telling a story helps overcome the challenges of understanding technology by shifting focus onto the results rather than the technology itself. Getting approval for marketing and promotional efforts, on the other hand, will likely require a more financially minded approach.

Many decision makers in the library industry look at marketing as a waste of library funds. It doesn't have a tangible benefit to patrons like services, materials, and programming do, so they feel they shouldn't spend money on it. That might have been somewhat true twenty years ago, before the Internet, social media, and instant access to practically everything. Now, that view is shortsighted.

In order for us to enter the consciousness of the people of our communities, we have to be where they are with content they will respond to. We can't just sit in our buildings and wait for them to show up. We have to make them curious about the library. We have to let them know what we have to offer and how it can benefit them. We have to give them a reason to want to use the library. And we have to be creative in our approach in order to accomplish these things.

For some decision makers, the very mention of the word *marketing*, for instance, might mean immediate rejection. For this reason, when discussing these ideas with them, try to avoid using words that might have negative connotations. Don't talk about advertising, or promoting, or even marketing. Talk to them about public awareness and outreach.

People are more comfortable with "making the public aware" than they are with "advertising." After all, one of our goals as institutions is to make our communities more aware of our services. We can't say one of our goals is advertising. We're trying to get decision makers to say "yes" to something *they* want to do.

Once you've framed the discussion palatably, focus on showing them how many people your idea has the potential to reach. In the billboard example we used in chapter 6, I discussed how to break down the cost of the billboard based on the amount of traffic passing by it daily:

> At CCJPL, the average drive-by traffic for one of our billboard locations is 25,000 people a day. Over the course of a year, that billboard will have been seen approximately 9,125,000 times. Each of our billboards costs $3,000 annually. That's $8.22 a day. At that rate, the library is spending $0.0003 per exposure opportunity.

You'll want to present your numbers in a particular order. In the example, I first presented the number of people who pass by the billboard on a daily basis, 25,000. Most people don't realize how many vehicles pass by any particular location every day. This is likely to be surprising to your decision makers. Next, I extrapolated that over an entire year. That's 9,125,000 people, an astounding number. With those kinds of numbers in their heads, the $3,000 cost seems rather small. Once that's broken down to $8.22 per day, it really looks inexpensive. Breaking it down even further, to $0.0003 per vehicle, it almost seems as though we're getting it for free. Decision makers appreciate and respond well to numerical evidence, which can immediately illustrate a project's value and ease their minds as they consider your idea.

Another challenging example is Facebook advertising. Some decision makers may not even have Facebook accounts and therefore be completely unfamiliar with how Facebook works. To them, it may just seem like some silly game on the Internet. Others may be active on Facebook but have no understanding of how the advertising process works. Worse yet, they may even consider the ads an annoyance.

You'll have to first do some explaining about what a Facebook ad is and how it works, which was covered in chapter 4. You'll still want to discuss your idea in terms of public awareness. You aren't advertising on Facebook. You're utilizing social media to increase public awareness of the library. Again, you're trying to make them comfortable with a new concept.

Even so, you're still going to have to talk about a Facebook ad, and call it such, because that's what it is. However, you might use an analogy to help decision makers become more comfortable with the concept.

Consider comparing your Facebook ad to posters you might hang up around town. Explain to your decision makers that it's the same concept, just on a different platform. People log onto Facebook, just like they go into restaurants and convenience stores. The posters you hang up around town are meant to catch people's attention and make them aware of events or services at the library. A Facebook ad does the same thing. As with the stories discussed in the previous section, you're making decision makers aware of what a Facebook ad does, rather than focusing on what it is.

Use the Freegal example from chapter 4 to show the value of a Facebook ad:

> A $50 Facebook ad will reach about 10,000 people. Free music is a pretty great offer, but we'll be conservative and say that 2 percent of the people who saw the ad went to our website and down-

loaded music (remember, 2.9 percent clicked on the ad to learn more about the concerts). That's 200 people.

Each of those people gets to download three songs. So, that's 600 songs downloaded. The average cost to download a song from iTunes, Amazon, or elsewhere is basically $1.00.

By running a $50 ad for a week, your library has saved your community $600. That's a substantial return on investment.

But that's just one week. What happens if those same people download their three songs for an entire year? That's 31,200 songs, or $31,200 in savings, from a $50 ad.

That's how the ad shows an ROI for the community. They are able to get the music for free from the library, rather than paying for it. Now let's look at how the ad shows an ROI for the library.

Freegal's contract requires the library to pay a flat rate annually and this was a good thing for the library. For this example, we'll say that our contract is $10,000 a year.

We'll also say we haven't done a great job of promoting the service and we're averaging about 10,000 downloads per year. (You may be doing better. This is an example. Just bear with me). So, we're basically paying the same price per song, $1.00, as our patrons would be paying if they bought the songs from iTunes. That's not being a very effective resource for our community. There's no value there.

Now let's factor in those 31,200 songs we got for our $50 ad. That would give us a total of 41,200 songs, while our contract is still $10,000. That works out to $0.24 per song, while increasing the value, the ROI, of our Freegal contract by over 300 percent. That's being a very effective resource for our community. Not bad, Facebook.

I'm well aware that I've made a lot of assumptions in this argument, and the numbers there aren't really attainable. But that's part of the beauty of the argument.

It doesn't matter if the boss tries to tell you not everyone is going to download all their songs every week, or not all 200 people who went to the website would have a library card, or not everyone who downloaded music would have otherwise bought it.

It's impossible for them to strip away enough value to say it isn't worth it to run the $50 ad. We're trying to help them do the right thing. We shouldn't really have to sell the idea to them. It's just math.

Using Facebook advertising as a public awareness tool can increase value in virtually any service we offer. Our ROI is value-based. We aren't a business. We're never going to show a profit. We measure our return on investment based on utilization. The more people who use our services, the more valuable those services become, both socially and financially.

All this talk about using the right words and or talking about costs in a certain way might seem sort of manipulative. But that isn't the case at all. You aren't doing anything conniving by choosing your words carefully or presenting your numbers in a particular way. It isn't that you're trying to put something over on your decision makers. It's not a trick. All you're doing is helping them understand the right thing to do in a way that's comfortable for them.

DEAR DECISION MAKER

I've had the privilege of working under extraordinary leadership during my time at CCJPL. Both Phyllis Burkett and David Eckert have been forward-thinking and adventurous directors, willing to try new things and always looking for ways to make our library better.

David maintains an open-door policy with everyone on staff. Anyone, with any idea, is welcome to come to him. He may say "yes" and he may say "no," but he will only do so after he fully understands the idea.

We're fortunate to also have a board that is just as forward-thinking as our administration. They were willing to believe in a vision early on and gave us an opportunity to take the library in a new, digital direction. Once they were able to see the results of our endeavors, they went from giving hesitant approval to becoming motivated advocates.

This isn't to say we never get told "no" by administration or the board. But they are always willing to *listen* and make the best-informed decision they can for the good of our library and community.

I can't tell you what sorts of ideas your team might bring to you or whether you should approve them or not. But I implore you to listen to them and genuinely consider their ideas before making a decision.

There are such things as bad ideas. Trust me. I have had my share of them. But if your staff is coming to you with strategies from this book, please give them your utmost consideration. The strategies in this book aren't radical. They are fundamental practices that are needed in any library looking to remain relevant and grow their audience in today's environment.

Once you've given your staff approval to move forward with one of these projects, also give them room to learn as they go. They're going to make mistakes along the way. Be constructive and continue to support them.

For instance, if you've approved the Facebook strategies from chapter 3, and a staff member puts up an evening post that inadvertently "crosses the line" and receives some negative comments from patrons, keep that in perspective. It's just one post and you can always take it down. Social media is short-attention-span theater. If your staff posts a warm and fuzzy picture the next night, all will be forgiven and forgotten.

What you don't want to do is have a knee-jerk reaction and decide you need to implement some draconian social media policy stating that only things directly related to the library can be posted. It not only kills the confidence of your staff, it also destroys the very mechanics that make the Facebook strategies successful.

Being a good leader means allowing your staff to fail with confidence. Provide an environment where they aren't beaten over the head when they make mistakes, but are instead picked back up, brushed back off, and encouraged to get out there and try again. Foster a culture of creativity.

By no means am I trying to tell you how to do your job. I'm in no way qualified to do that. What I am doing is asking you to give these strategies a chance. I've done my best to explain how they work and why they work. The very worst thing that can happen is you'll wind up having more people using the library.

NOTE: Because of the importance of understanding how to work with decision makers to get approval for your initiatives, I asked Carson Block, of Carson Block Consulting, to contribute his insights on the subject. Carson travels the country, working with library leaders to develop technology and management strategies for their organizations. His contribution can be found in appendix C.

8

START YOUR OWN REVOLUTION

WE'RE ALMOST DONE

I'm passionate about the work I do, and I truly love my library. It's like a child I've had the opportunity to help raise with the rest of my library family. The library has come so far over the past few years, and I am so proud of all the work we've put into it. I don't think I could ask for a better job or a better group of people to work with. I know the difference we're making in the lives of the people in our community. I get to be a witness to it every day.

I haven't always felt this way about libraries. Before I came to work at CCJPL, I didn't even have a library card. If you had asked me to tell you my most vivid memories of libraries, I could have only given you two.

THE STABBING

The first memory would have been when I was in fourth grade. I was sitting in the school library, minding my own business, when another boy stole a note being passed to me from a girl in our class. He and I argued back and forth across the table until I finally got angry enough that I threw my pencil at him.

I wasn't trying to hurt him. Don't get some mental picture of me going all psycho on a classmate with a pencil. It wasn't like that.

But the sharp end did catch him in the side of the head and a little blood started trickling down. When the kid next to him pointed this out, my wounded enemy went into a complete panic. His tears, snot, and vomit made the situation far worse than necessary.

My first memory of libraries ended with me getting a paddling from the principal. And no, I never did get the note from that girl.

FOLLOWING THE LIGHT

My second memory of libraries would have been from my freshman year of college. I was going through an experimental stage in life and playing the role of the hippie kid.

Late one experimental afternoon, as a friend and I strolled around campus, we wound up following a ray of sunlight shining onto the ground between the buildings. It was *important* that we find out where the light led. It became a mission, a quest, a pilgrimage.

As we walked from between two building and into the wide-open lawn in the center of campus, we looked up to see the sun setting just behind the library. In that moment, I *understood*. Euphorically, I proclaimed, "The light leads to the library."

Looking back twenty-something years later, perhaps the light did lead to the library after all. It just took me a while to get here.

OUR PATRONS, THEIR VIDEO

If asked today to list my most vivid memories of libraries, there would be too many to count. I've spent the last six years working in a magical place, with magical people who do magical things. But there are a couple of special memories that help remind me of what it really means to work in a library.

Early on in our YouTube series, we had to shoot a couple of scenes for our second video that required some extras. We were shooting near the public computers, so I announced what we were doing and asked who wanted to be in a video. Several of the volunteers were regular patrons who stayed at the homeless shelter down the street. It only took us an hour or so to shoot everything we needed, and then everyone went back to what they were doing.

A couple of weeks later, I completed editing the video and posted it on YouTube. I went out into the public computer area and showed the folks who'd been in the video how to access it. For the next few weeks, every time I'd walk through the public computers, I'd see at least one of them watching *their* video.

Their total screen time in the video wasn't more than a few seconds, but that didn't matter. It was theirs. That's when I realized what a sense of ownership means to someone who has nothing.

One day, one of the patrons from the video asked me if I could help him real quick. I asked him what he needed and he told me he wanted me to show him how to send the video in an e-mail. He wanted to send it to his family, just to let them know he was okay. I was starting to learn what it meant to work in a library.

FAMILY

Every year at our library, we have a Genealogy Night Lock-in. It's a night when we stay open until midnight and allow our local genealogists to geek on ancestry. In 2012 a lady showed up for genealogy night because she'd seen one of our posters. She approached Nancy Matthews, a member of our local Genealogy Society, and asked for help.

The lady's parents had passed away and after their death, she'd learned that they weren't actually her biological parents. She was trying to find out about her birth parents. Nancy took her back to a group of genealogists who spent the evening trying to put together the puzzle of this lady's past with what little information she had to work from.

Using the information she acquired at the library that night, she came to learn that she'd been stolen from the hospital at birth. Eventually, she managed to find out who her birth parents were and was reunited with a family she never knew she had. She saw a poster, and came to a library, and asked for help.

FAREWELL

These are the reasons we do what we do. We aren't in the library industry for the money. It doesn't pay that well. We're here because somewhere along the way, we realized we could make a difference in people's lives by working in a library.

I'm not a writer. I'm just a tech guy who knows a little bit about people. I don't know whether you've learned anything from me or not, but I've done my part. I wrote the book. What happens next is up to you. Now go out and start your own revolution. #makeithappen

It's the only way it can work.
Or nostalgia will murder us all and
walk grinning into our funerals.

—JOSH HANAGARNE,
BORROWING FROM KHALIL GIBRAN

APPENDIX A

TWITTER

Ned Potter

GETTING THE MOST OUT OF TWITTER

Twitter.com is, at the time of writing, the second most popular social network in the world. It's behind Facebook, of course, but in my view there is a stronger overlap with the kinds of people who use libraries and the kinds of people who tweet, than with any other social media.

Why should you be on there? Twitter users are receptive to interacting with libraries on the platform. They want to hear from us, and they want us to listen to them. For me, it's the first place to start when building your library's social media portfolio; get Twitter right, and the rest becomes so much easier. You can boost your reputation, you can reach new audiences, you can engage existing customers and you can really show some personality. Twitter is the chance to be open and approachable and informal, without losing credibility or authority.

So how do you get the most out of it? Here are ten bite-sized tips, divided into two sections. The first section is "Getting Started"—what are the foundations of establishing a great Twitter account? Then we move on to "Going Further." A lot of library Twitter accounts start off full of optimism and freshness, but then reach a plateau a half-year or so in, where the followers, the level of engagement, and the return on your time investment stops going up. There are ways to get over this hump, some of which I've detailed below. Once you get past the plateau your momentum will become self-sustaining and your network will grow and grow.

If you're not yet familiar with Twitter, there's a whole set of terms and phrases that are associated with the platform that may not make much sense to you. I've included a brief glossary of the key terms at the end of this case study, so skip to that if you need a primer before reading the advice below.

GETTING STARTED

1. **Don't tell people you're there until you've done some groundwork.**
    Once you've set up your account, don't start following people and tweeting right away, or you may miss out on some important opportunities. Whenever you follow someone on Twitter, they get a notification telling them so—chances are, when they see this, they'll click on your profile and make a three-second decision on whether to follow you back. This will be based on your profile and your last few tweets. If they don't follow you back it's not the end of the world, but it greatly reduces the chances of meaningful conversation later down the road, so it pays to get the foundations right before you launch. With this in mind: put in a proper picture. Twitter users hate the default "egg" avatar, and they'll assume you're a spam account if you keep it. Find a picture (of your logo or your library) that works in the very small size at which it will appear in peoples' time lines. Put in a proper bio. And that doesn't mean something like "The official Twitter account of Library X!"—anyone reading your bio should already know from your name who you are. Use the bio to give them a *reason* to follow you, such as "Tweeting about culture, technology, books, and upcoming events at the Library." Once your avatar and bio are sorted and you've put in a link to your library's website, write a few tweets. It feels silly tweeting before you have an audience, but people need to see some kind of representation of your style. Write four or five tweets. *Then*, and only then, start following people and otherwise telling your users and potential users you're there.

2. **Go for an informal tone.**
    Libraries often struggle with this at first, but if you can, try and be colloquial, approachable, and informal, without being self-consciously wacky or otherwise losing credibility. Don't be afraid to use "I" rather than "the Library" even though you're tweeting as the organization— Twitter is a conversation, so people expect to be conversing with a person behind the account.

3. **Remember Twitter is a conversation, not a broadcast.**

I really can't emphasize this enough—social media is participatory and interactive, so be prepared for a two-way conversation on Twitter. You can tweet announcements, sure, but also tweet questions—and *listen* to the answers; listening is so important. In fact, in an ideal world, a rule of thumb to aim for is one in four tweets are broadcasts, the other three being replies, Retweets, or links to third-party content, which is potentially useful to your followers but not necessarily directly related to your library.

GOING FURTHER

1. **Ask questions.**

As a general rule, the more interactive a library Twitter account is, the more popular it will become. Responding to questions your users ask you on Twitter as soon as possible is really important—but so is starting conversations yourself. Ask your followers for book recommendations, or their favorite apps, or their top tips for using the library—then Retweet the best answers for everyone to see.

2. **Tweet multimedia.**

Entirely text-based tweets are fine, but why stop there? Twitter embeds most multimedia in your Tweet, meaning that it can be viewed or watched on Twitter itself without your followers having to leave the site. Links to YouTube videos, Prezi and Slideshare presentations, plus pictures via Twitpic, will magically make the objects appear in your tweet. If you're tweeting about something happening in your library, take a pic on your phone and tweet that too. It'll get much more traction that way. Pictures of displays, of workshops and classes, new decoration—even print screens of websites you're linking to.

3. **If something is important, tweet it four times.**

As you might expect, only a relatively small percentage of your followers are online at any one time—so you need to tweet important information and links across a period of two days and covering different times of day (and schedule a midnight tweet too if you have international followers in different time zones). If it's a link to a blog post, rather than just tweeting the title each time, tweet a key piece of information or quote from the post—this stops your time line being filled with duplicate tweets, and hooks people in over time.

4. **Get Retweeted and your network will grow.**

   When someone Retweets (RTs) your tweet, it appears in their profile, viewable by all their followers. So nothing gets you new followers like tweeting something great and having loads of people Retweet it—it exposes your tweet and your Twitter presence to several new networks at once, some of whom may well be inspired to check you out and follow you. The best way to get RTs is to be *useful*, to tweet really punchy tips or advice or links. You're also more likely to be Retweeted if you show some personality. What else can you do to make it more likely?

   First, simply ask people to RT. If you say "Please RT!" you will get ten times the number of RTs you would otherwise. If you spell it out—"Please Retweet!" you will get twenty-three times as many! But you can only use this very sparingly—when something is *really* important or *really* useful. If you abuse people's kindness they'll soon switch off and stop RTing. Another thing to keep in mind is, if possible, leave an RT space. By which I mean, if you can express yourself in, say, 100 characters rather than the full 140, that allows someone wanting to manually Retweet you some space to add their own comment or endorsement.

5. **Analyze your tweets.**

   There are a million and one packages that promise you some statistical insight into your Twitter account—the trick is finding the ones whose information you can *act* on. Stick your Library's Twitter handle into www.tweetstats.com and check out how many of your tweets are replies and RTs—if the combined total is below 25 percent you need to make an active effort to change this; once you do, your network will grow. Tweetstats will also tell you when you tweet, which allows you to know (rather than guess) whether your followers are getting a consistent level of service across the week. If all your tweets happen at 9 a.m. (when "the person who tweets" gets into work and thinks, hmm, better do my tweeting for the day), then you need to change that. Combine information about when you tweet with the information www.tweriod.com

gives you about when your followers are online, and you can start to really use Twitter in a focused, targeted, and successful way.

6. **Use Twitter for social monitoring.**

   People will be talking about your library on Twitter, and it's always useful to know what they're saying. Those who know you're on the network may speak directly to you using your @ name, but you can also pick up on conversations that aren't addressed to you. Run a search for your library's name, plus any shortenings commonly used. You can then save those searches and run them each day to pick up relevant tweets. You can also set up a location search on the word *library*—to pick up any tweets within, say, one mile of your location, to catch people who say things like "I'm in the library, can't find the journals!" and reply with help and guidance. Investigate Twitter's Advanced Search functionality for more options.

7. **Put your Twitter handle *everywhere*.**

   Although using Twitter is in itself marketing, you still need to market the marketing . . . People need to know you're on the platform at all, so tell them—put your user name on bookmarks, leaflets, and handouts, put it on staff members' business cards, embed your tweet-stream on your library home page, have a live tweet-stream on your digital display screens for a day. You're putting the effort in to be there, so shout loudly about your activity!

Enjoy your Twitter activity, have fun with it. Don't get too caught up in the numbers—it's not about how many followers you have (although more is better, generally), it's about having some kind of *impact* using social media. A library Twitter account with 5,000 followers who are completely passive is worth much less than one with 1,000 followers whose *behavior has been changed* by the Twitter account—people who use the library more often, more effectively, or who praise it to their networks and RT your tweets. Above all Twitter is about engagement.

Good luck!

@theREALwikiman

A BRIEF GLOSSARY

Username. This is what you are called on Twitter, and all user names are prefixed by @—it's best to keep yours relatively short.

Profile. Your Twitter profile is what other people see when they click on your user name—it consists of your user name, your actual name, a profile picture, a background picture, a short bio (160 characters), and a link to a website of your choosing; it's important to make the most of all these.

Tweet. The tweet is the public message itself, displayed online. It is also a verb (I'm going to tweet about this; I tweeted about that). A tweet is viewable by anyone who clicks on your profile, although in practice it will only be seen by those who follow you. You will also hear the term *Tweeter* to refer to people who tweet.

Time line. Your time line is what you see when you log into Twitter—by default you'll be on the Home screen, which consists of your own tweets, tweets from people you follow, and Retweets. The @Connect screen shows you tweets directed specifically at you, the tweets of yours that are Retweeted or Favorited, plus information about when new people follow you. The #Discover screen is an attempt to expose you to other Twitter activity based on your interests—in practice this will be the screen you use the least, if at all.

Reply/@/Mentions. Users can Tweet directly at another user to converse and ensure their replies appear in the other users' time line. As long as a Tweet has someone's @user name in, they should see it.

RT (or Retweet). To Retweet someone is essentially to quote them—clicking the Retweet button will cause their Tweet to appear in your time line, so you'll be sharing it with all your followers. You can also "manually" Retweet by typing "RT," then the original Tweeter's name, then their Tweet. This allows you to add your own comment in at the start, prior to the Retweeted text.

Follow/Unfollow. This is the basis of the Twitter network. If you Follow someone you see their Tweets (and those they Retweet; see below) in your time line; if they follow you, they see your Tweets. It's a good idea to Follow plenty of relevant people so you have a steady stream of information and content, but it's also okay to "prune" and unfollow people or organizations over time if they cease to be relevant—following too many people can make Twitter less useful to you.

MT (or Modified Tweet). As above, but you're editing the Tweet so it is no longer a verbatim quote. This is generally done to shorten the Tweet to allow you more room for your own comment—if you edit the Tweet at all from the original source, you should use MT rather than RT.

DM (or Direct Message). A Direct Message is a private message sent between users; it does not appear on the network. It's important to note that only people you follow can DM you (and you can only DM people who follow you). Therefore tweets like "New internship available at the library—DM us for details" are a bad idea, because not everyone reading the Tweet will actually be able to message you.

Favorite. Any Tweet can be Favorited by clicking the little star below it—this means it is in effect filed for later use, via your Favorites screen. This is useful for keeping track of useful tweets or links, flagging something to respond to later when you have more time, or collating responses to a particular Tweet. It is also useful to see which of your own Tweets are Favorited, as the fact that a fellow Twitter user has taken an action based on your output is indicative of some kind of impact.

APPENDIX B

PINTEREST

Josh Tate

I N THREE YEARS, Pinterest has become one of the larger social media sites. It has 70 million users who spend an average of 98 minutes per month pinning. Most of Pinterest's users are women, and about half have children. The site has become so successful that it has changed how many companies design their websites, compelling them to add more graphics and images.[1]

Pinterest's popularity and its target demographics, which are in line with traditional library users, make it an exciting potential new marketing vehicle for libraries. Therefore, libraries are increasingly evaluating if their organization should start a Pinterest account.

WHAT IS PINTEREST?

Pinterest is an online visual filing system, or virtual pin-board, that allows users to organize and share images. Much like visual bookmarks, Pinterest is a way to keep all the little visual things a person finds on the Internet saved and organized in one place and creates a storage site for those ideas and inspirations.

Pinterest is extremely visual and revolves around serendipitous discovery. The site consists of thousands of images, or pins, presented on either one main page (a user's Home Feed) or arranged into categories, that can then be searched, organized, and shared. Using Pinterest consists of scrolling through page after page of images and adding them to user-defined groups, or boards. The real attraction to Pinterest is that users create their own boards to organize and arrange Pinterest's vast image collections to suit their needs and imaginations. As all boards are user-generated, it provides tremendous flexibility and customization, allowing for users to create boards on "Future Trips," "Awesome '80s," "Wedding Ideas," "Must-Have Fashions," "Hot Guys," and more.

Pinterest is also a social media site, allowing users to share their images with others on Pinterest or by connecting through Facebook or Twitter. Users can follow other Pinterest accounts, which automatically adds pins from these accounts to the user's Home Feed. Following an account makes it easy to discover new pins from a user's favorite Pinterest accounts or boards. Further, users can also "like" another user's pin or make a comment on one of their boards.

SHOULD THE LIBRARY USE PINTEREST?

Whether to start a library Pinterest account will depend in large part on your library's overall social media strategy. If the library is still struggling to create a Facebook or Twitter presence, creating another social media channel may not be advantageous and could take away resources from those pursuits. The objective of using social media is to be part of and engaged in the same places as your customers. A primary goal with Pinterest should be to enhance or supplement other social media sites, as the return on investment for Pinterest is more ambiguous than with other sites. Therefore, the main question to ask is if Pinterest fits the library's social media strategy or overall strategic plan and library mission?

If your library has a good social media policy or library mission statement, there are still a few questions to answer before making a final determination:

■ How much staff time is available for pinning? (Hint: it won't take very much.)

Even with a strong social media policy in place, Pinterest will consume staff time. Decide how much time staff will be available to pin. It doesn't take much time per day, particularly if your organization already use images in library marketing and online. A good Pinterest page will typically change out each board's cover, or add five new images per board, each week. This translates to roughly 5–10 minutes per board per week.

Pinterest is also one of those sites where more people participating and adding content will help create a better product. Serendipity is key to Pinterest, where users are accustomed to perusing a wide variety of images and pinning to a large number of disparate boards. If you can get multiple staff pinning, it will help your Pinterest account's diversity and save staff time by dispersing the overall load. However, you will want to assign one person to help keep all the pinners organized, or act as the project manager for the Pinterest account.

- Who in your organization will pin? Do you have any Pinthusiasts you can use?

  Luckily, you probably already have your best Pinterest resource, Pinthusiasts. One of the easiest ways to begin planning and use Pinterest in your library is to find those people in your organization who are already using the site and are enthusiastic about Pinterest, or your Pinthusiasts. Pinterest users are vocal, passionate, and dedicated. Your library can use this passion and current involvement to quickly find staff to help with planning or start a pilot project. Furthermore, Pinthusiasts will give your Pinterest account the authenticity you need to engage customers. Pinthusiasts want to use Pinterest; they are not just doing it as part of their job!

  In addition, Pinterest has a collaboration feature that lets staff pin to a library Pinterest board using their personal Pinterest account. The collaboration feature allows your Pinthusiasts to easily incorporate pinning for the library into their normal Pinterest use. With the collaboration feature, there is no need to share passwords or master account information.

- Are there partners in the local or national community to collaborate with on content?

  With the collaboration feature your library can also coordinate with other libraries, local businesses, or organizations to create community boards that the library sponsors. Many organizations even use Pinterest to collaborate internally, such as a Youth Services Pinterest board for story-time ideas. However it's used, collaborating can provide an additional incentive to create a Pinterest account.

- Does your library incorporate imagery on your website and in your organization's marketing, or will you need to create images?

Finally, Pinterest is all about images. While you can post some text, such as inspirational quotes, the most popular pins are images or images with text. If your organization's current marketing and website design strategies include lots of images, it will decrease the time staff spends pinning library materials. If your library doesn't have a strong design element, you will need to plan more time for staff to create images to promote your library's content.

STRATEGIES FOR PINNING

There is no need to reinvent the wheel when setting up your library's Pinterest account. Libraries are already arranged in collections, categories, or genres and librarians already provide recommendation services such as reader's advisory. It is simply a matter of translating these library-defined collections and services into a more Pinterest-friendly format.

Once you have a small group of Pinthusiasts eager to pin for the library, you need to decide what kind of content you will provide. Start by creating a pinning strategy or a formal document that describes in general what types of content staff should pin and the theme and goal of each of your Pinterest boards. A pinning strategy will allow you to have multiple staff pinning, yet keep quality consistent and provide accountability if staff fail to meet objectives. A good beginning strategy for board creation and pinning content is to focus on promoting the library, the library experience, and library staff.

Pins and boards should help to promote the library's collections, programs, services, and other digital content when possible. Books, program photographs, blog posts, and service videos are a few of the many types of library content available to pin. If it has a graphic component it can be used on Pinterest, including the library's catalog through pinning book covers.

Pins and boards should also promote the "library experience." Let your staff use their judgment as library employees and pin items that reflect the core values of the library and pin on topics that your customers might find interesting, enjoyable, or educational. These pins are related to your collections, but are not images or items found in those collections.

Your boards and pins may be related to your in-house collections, but to get the most engagement and return on investment from customers, your library should use Pinterest just like your customers do. A good way to view a Pinterest board is as a collection of staff picks on a variety of topics. In essence, each board is stating "here are things we think you will like," but on more than just books or materials owned by the library.

For example, if you have a cooking or food-related board, allow staff to post nonlibrary pins such as recipes, food images, cooking techniques, and so on that they find on Pinterest. Don't force a marketing strategy onto Pinterest. Rather, use Pinterest the way your customers do, allowing for a more organic and natural experience.

Finally, Pinterest is not just about the library and its collections. It's about creating a real customer experience. Therefore, pins should also promote your library's staff. Use the pins and boards to reflect their personality and show the wonderful and diverse nature of the library's staff. Pinterest is about having fun, so let your staff express that.

PINTEREST BOARD PLANNING

Following your pinning strategy will help in creating your Pinterest boards. Each board should have an initial goal and description that staff and patrons can use to determine if a pin fits into that board. For the initial launch of your organization's account, the general rule of thumb is 8 to 12 boards. This may seem like a large amount of content, but remember that Pinterest users are used to navigating through lots of images and content. It's a natural part of the Pinterest experience.

Also remember that Pinterest users tend to be predominately women aged 24–35, half of whom have children. Although you want to target all of your customers with Pinterest, make sure to pay particular attention to your core users when creating boards.

Using the general strategies for pinning, a few good boards to start include:

- *Staff Picks*—Pin images from your catalog with a brief, Tweetable review or reason for inclusion. Include boards for books, movies, music, and any other formats you circulate. These boards are reflections of traditional library tools, but they remain popular and effective engagement tools.

- *Special or Unique Collections at the Library*—If your organization is known for its local history collection, be sure to include a board promoting it.

- *Library Programming Board*—You can create one general programming promotion board or create individual boards for different programs. Summer Reading boards tend to be popular individual programming boards.

- *Boards on Popular Patron Topics*—The more common topics pinned on Pinterest include food, health, fashion, children, travel, and home decor. Chances are that your customers will also enjoy boards about these subjects. Again, use your pinning strategy to move away from strict marketing to include non-library materials in these boards.

- *A Just-for-Fun Board*—This is a board for staff to pin interesting or fun images they find on Pinterest. Some of the more successful and popular library boards are those where staff post random images they find interesting. Let your staff's personality shine here.

STRATEGY FOR SETTING UP THE PAGE

After determining the starting boards and pinning strategy, setting up the account is straightforward. While you can simply sign up the library as an individual account, Pinterest has a special account option for businesses and nonprofit entities called Pinterest for Businesses. Pinterest for Businesses offers the same Pinterest experience as an individual account but offers a variety of extra tools to help you integrate Pinterest into your library's website and get the most return from your account.

A few things to keep in mind when building your Pinterest page:

- Verify your organization's website on Pinterest. Pinterest provides a way to verify your Pinterest account, which allows users to quickly tell they are on the organization's official site.

- Make sure to include branding and organizational description information, including your logo.

- Use an organizational e-mail, such as pinterest@yourlibrary.org, when setting up the account. You do not want to tie the library's Pinterest account to one person's e-mail.

- If you have more than one person pinning, create a Pinterest e-mail user group to allow for better communication.

- In each board description, include your library name to ensure someone coming to that board knows they are on the library's account. This practice is just another way to ensure your branding is successful.

- Each pin should link back to the library directly with a URL, or indirectly with some reference to the library.

- Make board names fun! Avoid library lingo whenever possible.

- Add the *Pin It button* to your website. The *Pin It button* is provided by Pinterest and allows your website users to quickly share your content via Pinterest much like other social media buttons found on websites.

- A board cover consists of five images. Make sure to have at least five pins in a board to prevent its looking empty.

- Add new content to your boards daily or at least weekly. Fresh content will keep your images in your follower's home feed, making your content more visible and discoverable while keeping your account relevant to customers.

- Have one person control the main library account, such as to create the initial boards, add new boards, update organization information, and so on.

- Follow those patrons who have followed you. If a patron takes the time to follow one or more of your boards, it is considered proper social media etiquette to follow them in return. However, if the follower is outside your organization's geographic area, or is another institution you shouldn't follow them.

ROI AND STATISTICS

Return on investment for Pinterest is less tangible than other library services. Pinterest does have built-in analytics that allow you to track the number of repins (when another Pinterest user pins something you've pinned), clicks, most-pinned items, and several other data points. Of the data provided, tracking the number of followers tends to be the most widely used metric when looking at return on investment. If your account routinely attracts new followers, it's a good sign your site is connecting with customers and growing.

Followers are people who are actively watching what you pin to your Pinterest page. These are the patrons who are most engaged on your site and will see what you pin. Unfortunately, Pinterest does not provide much information about those followers, such as demographics, which would aid in tailoring board content. Also, this user data does not necessarily translate into direct library use. Your library may have 500 followers on Pinterest, but this may not translate into 500 users of the physical library or website.

Therefore, it is important to remember that Pinterest is not just about marketing the library, but engaging users. If users like what they see on your library's Pinterest account, they'll stay followers and repin your images, which keeps the library in the forefront of users' online awareness. Pins may not lead to a direct increase in circulation, but a good Pinterest presence will keep your customers aware of the library when they are online. Customers will then make a point of looking for your pins in their home feeds, giving you one of those intangibles of marketing, visibility. That online situational awareness can be invaluable as the demand for customers' attention increases.

Overall, creating a Pinterest presence for your library is not difficult with a little planning. Look at your social media strategy, your library's mission, the number of staff you can commit to the project, and determine how your library can best use this social media site. Start a pilot project focusing on a pinning strategy that incorporates pins about your collections, the library experience, and your staff. Then find and unleash your organization's Pinthusiasts and become part of an exciting new social media experiment for libraries!

NOTE

1. B. Honigman, *100 Fascinating Social Media Statistics and Figures from 2012*, November 29, 2012, HuffingtonPost.com: www.huffingtonpost.com/brian-honigman/100 -fascinating-social-me_b_2185281.html.

APPENDIX C

MORE CONVINCING THE DECISION MAKERS

Carson Block

GETTING THE GREEN LIGHT:
SOME STRATEGIC TIPS FOR MOVING DECISION MAKERS TO "YES"

It can start like this: a compelling vision burning itself into your brain, and sometimes all the way through to your fingers on a keyboard. Or perhaps wrapped around whatever writing implement is at hand on any scrap of paper you can scrounge, including that empty fast-food bag tumbling around on the floor of your car. These moments have also been known to be captured on the proverbial cocktail napkin. The moment of inspiration doesn't care what tools (if any) you have to capture it. It is here, by golly, and you better pay attention.

So you do. In a flash you not only see the impact you want to have, but also the route you will take. You see the potential hurdles and how to route around them. You can also clearly see what resources you need. It's doable—it's all doable! This can be real!

And your next thought is "If only '*they*' would let me do this, it would change the world, or at least our library."

It's at this point that many incredibly great, life-altering ideas die a stillborn death. The idea of having to secure permission—and better yet support—for your idea makes you freeze in your tracks. "I get it," you think to yourself. "My friends will get it. But how will I make *them* get it?" In almost diametric opposition to the passion powering your inspiration, you shrink at the thought of having to (ugh) *explain* its awesomeness. Your shoulders go from broad to sunken. "Maybe this isn't such a great idea after all," you think to yourself as you try to reconcile your great passion with the next step in bringing it to life. You are now at a point of decision that is just as important as the original inspiration. Will you go forward—or will you drop it?

Unfortunately it's not enough to just be inspired—you also need to make it happen.

Of course, the scenario above may not reflect your own experiences. For some, moving decision makers to "yes" is a walk in the park. These people seem to be born with the skills and intestinal fortitude to consistently get their ideas on the table. If that describes you—move along citizen; there is probably nothing for you to see here. For others, though—those who need a little help in bridging inspiration with all of the actions required to make it happen—read on.

WHAT'S THE SECRET TO SUCCESS?

The secret to success in convincing decision makers isn't as much a mystery as it is good old elbow grease. It begins with really knowing what you want to accomplish and articulating it clearly. It is brought to life through a combination of skills, strategy, technique, and endurance—and lacking any of those, single-minded and sloppy determination will do just fine. It's more than just "selling it" but also bringing it to life. One without the other is just puffery; the two together create a promise kept.

In the pursuit of "yes," your goal is to play cupid and help your decision maker or makers fall in love with the idea just as much as you have.

We often refer to this concept as getting someone "on board"—and I think what we most often mean by that phrase is something that goes beyond a simple acknowledgment or agreement, but a deep and shared commitment and belief in the new project, service, or effort: the sorts of commitment that will cause a decision maker to join, support, and happily embrace the entire journey from idea to execution to impact—the sort of belief that will drive your decision makers to champion your work within their circles of friends and colleagues, and evangelize your ideas in areas only they have access to.

SETTING YOUR CONTEXT

In this book, Ben Bizzle is talking about efforts involving technology and marketing in libraries—two areas that have come into our operations like a thief in the night. In the not-too-distant past, both were interesting but often considered nonessential to the library.

Today, we must start with the assumption that technology (which is just one set of tools to accomplish our goals) permeates every aspect of library operations, and that marketing (which can simply be telling our story) should be fundamental to our daily efforts.

But what if your decision makers don't share that assumption? Having a shared understanding is essential, so if your decision makers don't understand—or worse, don't agree—with the role of technology and marketing in libraries, that's where you need to start. Tread carefully here—although it's likely that you are already immersed in these worlds; try not to assume the other person is a Luddite or out of touch with the modern world. There are legitimate reasons to be cautious about the use of technology, and some have had bad enough experiences with marketing that they consider it a four-letter word.

KNOW YOUR AUDIENCE

Let's back up for a second. Who are your decision makers? This is a good thing to think through—and perhaps chart out. Start with your own boss, of course, but also including the library director (if the director isn't already your supervisor), trustees, board members, city council members, and any others. Who needs to be looped in, and how? Even if your primary contact is your boss, thinking through this sphere of influence will help strategize a successful run at clearing the path for your ideas and efforts.

After getting your immediate decision maker or makers on board, a supporting strategy is thinking through what they need to solicit support from those in their circles—including their own supervisors, colleagues, constituents, and friends. Generally this includes equipping them with talking points—or simply stated concepts that help them quickly characterize and illustrate what you are doing—or what you want to do.

SMALL TALK

One approach is to think in terms of building relationships with your decision makers—and using a number of informal, casual conversations to explore the topics. In this way you can make it safe for your decision makers to share their own opinions, and create the opportunity to bring more information to the table—the sort of information they might need to really understand and get behind your efforts.

Through these conversations, your goal should be to build a shared purpose with your decision makers. Not only will you have a chance to give them more information about what you want to do—but you will also have the golden opportunity to learn about their needs, including their own vision, goals, agendas, and political pressures. Once you learn what these factors are, you can refine your approach to create the classic win-win situation.

KNOW YOUR TALKING POINTS

For the following tips, let's say that you're looking to get approval to use a specific social media platform to raise awareness of the library in the community. You have a key problem, though—your decision maker doesn't use social media, and therefore doesn't really understand it.

Your assignment is now simple—you need to help them understand the key elements of social media. Try this:

Answer these questions—in this sequence—for yourself. Challenge yourself to create concise, clear answers that any layperson can understand.

- What are social media, and who uses them?

- Why are social media important in our society?

- Why are libraries using social media, and how do they typically use them?

- Why do you want to use social media—and what do you specifically hope to accomplish?

The answers to these questions are now your talking points for your conversation—whether it happens in a series of small informal conversations, or in a single sitting—even formal ones such as trustee meetings or a presentation to your boss.

ARTICULATE CLEARLY WHAT YOUR IDEA IS AND ISN'T

This is also known as setting appropriate expectations. Even those with limited experiences with social media have heard about marketing campaigns that have "gone viral"—messages that grew from reaching just a few people and then mushroomed to millions across the globe. How often does that really happen? Maybe it's likely in your case—and maybe it's not—but it's up to you to set reasonable expectations. Decision makers should understand that whether you're creating a new website, starting a marketing campaign, or building a social media audience, results don't happen overnight. Don't underemphasize the importance of your idea, but don't set yourself up for failure with unrealistic projections either.

LOVE THE HATERS

You're likely to meet some resistance when introducing new ideas, such as social media marketing. When you encounter resistance, be sure to have a conversation with the person or people who don't like it. Explore with them what they're concerned about. Many times, if someone isn't a social medium user, they don't see how it can be an effective marketing tool. In that case, you'll want to show some real examples of how it can be used effectively. In other cases, they might be concerned about the two-way communication social media tends to bring up. Some folks are afraid of direct feedback. Again, this is an opportunity to immerse your audience—maybe invite them to participate with you using social media if they haven't used them before. Let them experience its value for themselves.

HAVE YOU PICKED THE RIGHT TOOL FOR THE RIGHT JOB?

To a hammer, every problem resembles a nail. Another assumption about "getting someone on board" is that his or her resistance is wrong. But actually, it may be quite right. Don't invalidate other ideas before considering their value. We're all capable of making mistakes or having our ideas improved upon. Always be willing to adapt, or even abandon, an idea if offered valid reasons why it won't work.

PLANS ARE USELESS; PLANNING IS INDISPENSABLE

A final word about accomplishing goals: as someone who leads and participates in a lot of planning efforts in libraries, one of my favorite quotes comes from President Dwight D. Eisenhower: "In preparing for battle I have found that plans are useless, but planning is indispensable." What I take from that quote is that the most important part of a plan is having the vision of what you can accomplish. The discipline involved in creating the path to the goal is also mightily important—it forces us to consider scenarios and commit to thoughts, actions, and deadlines. Sometimes, though, we find that the road we thought would get us there isn't heading in the right direction (this is when the "plan" can be "useless"). It is okay to abandon the wrong path to pick the right one that gets you to your goal. Be flexible. One person can't accomplish everything alone. Remain open to the ideas of others and collaborate with them in your shared quest to build a better library.

INDEX

f denotes figures

A

AirPAC, 6, 47
ALA Think Tank (Facebook), 89–90
Allen, Jeannie, 89
"app experience" pages, 53
apps, 42–43, 44
art typography theme, 126
attention, capturing, 123
audiobooks, 47

B

banned books, 64–65
barriers to entry, 26, 41
billboards, 124–126
Block, Carson, 161
body typeface, 144
Book Club, 63
bookmarks, 130–131
Box, Joe, 4, 5, 12, 14, 60, 61, 63, 64, 69, 71
branch pages, 48–49, 49*f*
branding, 140–141
Brightwell, Micah, 19, 71, 102, 107
Brightwell, Wade, 19, 70
Browning, Brian, 114
Burkett, Phyllis, 3–4, 8–9, 14, 19, 59, 65, 154, 160

C

calendar of events, 34–36, 35*f*, 50
Carroll, Valerie, 11, 12, 20, 62–63, 64
catalog
    on mobile website, 47
    on website, 30–31
censorship, 64–65

children's storytimes, 51
click-through-rate, 101
coasters, 131–133, 132*f*
color, 28, 146–147
community awareness, 8
community news, 120–122
"Computers in Libraries" conference, 5, 14
consistency, 8–9, 141
content management systems (CMSs), 25–26
Corter, Jim, 154
Craighead County Jonesboro Public Library (CCJPL)
    development of creative team for, 8–12
    eCard theme for, 12–15, 12–16, 123, 123*f*, 143*f*, 148*f*, 149
    site redesign for, 3–8
    successes of, 16–20
    WORDS campaign for, 67–68, 69*f*, 126, 127*f*
Crooked Valley Regional Library, 59

D

Darley, Nina, 19, 68
databases, mobile websites and, 49
decision makers
    advice for, 160–161
    convincing, 153–161, 185–190
    talking points for, 188
Dempsey, Kathy, 18
design, 139–151, 142*f*
digital services, 33–34
direct mailers, 130
display typeface, 144
Dowd, Nancy, 14, 18

BEN BIZZLE is the director of technology at Craighead County Jonesboro Public Library in Jonesboro, Arkansas. He is a 2013 *Library Journal* Marketing Mover and Shaker and part of Craighead County Jonesboro Public Library's 2013 John Cotton Dana Award-winning creative team. He is also a national speaker, library marketing consultant, and the founder of LibraryMarket.com. Bizzle attended the University of Memphis in Memphis, Tennessee, and after college he pursued a career in sales and management before transitioning to the technology field in the late 1990s. Prior to joining the library team, Bizzle spent seven years as a technologist in the health care industry, eventually becoming the director of information technology, responsible for the technology infrastructure for four hospitals in Arkansas, Alabama, and Georgia.

Since joining Craighead County Jonesboro Public Library in 2008, Bizzle has focused on virtualizing library resources and extending the library's reach beyond the library itself. He has developed a number of cost-effective ways to enhance the patron experience and increase community awareness of the value of public libraries.

MARIA FLORA is an award-winning journalist and writer who resides in Brookland, Arkansas, with her husband, also a writer, and their two Australian Shepherds. She has raised two children, including a librarian.